THE YOUNG LEADER

Fifty Essential Lessons to Influence & Inspire

a New Generation of Leaders

Mark Daniel Cohen

Illustrations by Sam Sellers

MONUMENTAL

M

PUBLISHING

The views expressed in this book are solely those of the author in his personal capacity.

Library of Congress Cataloging-in-Publication Data applied for.
ISBN-10: 0-692-35923-0
ISBN-13: 978-069-235923-5

Dedication

Thank you to Tim for your patience and the space
you allow me to pursue my passions, including the
writing of this book.

Thank you to my kids, Steven, Kristy, and Ryan,
for the pure joy you bring to my life.

Contents

Preface

In the fall of 2001, I arrived at JFK airport from Los Angeles—a young Red Cross volunteer responding to the worst attack on the United States since World War II. Away from my day job, I trained as a public affairs worker and for several years assisted in the aftermath of hurricanes, tornadoes, and fires. But 9/11 was something different...with so many lives lost and a city and nation, injured, shocked, and emboldened. In public affairs we communicate messages, raise awareness, and tell important stories. There was so much to do.

I was anxious to help, but not particularly self-confident alongside older, more seasoned relief workers. They were a steadfast, tireless, unflinching group of individuals. Then there were the teams we worked with at the various aid sites—heroes, all: recovery workers, firefighters, social workers, and a multitude of other government and agency staff. They were generous with their time and possessed seemingly boundless energy. They were full of courage as they slowly and deliberately moved rubble, out, and a sense of hope, in. Finally, then, we were surrounded by those calling New York City home—individuals I found spirited, determined, even welcoming.

I was humbled to live and work in that place and at that time, and I labored harder than I ever had to prove that I could be the sort of person who might succeed with a big challenge. I think I did okay...no more, no less. It was occasionally overwhelming, with many disconsolate tears shed in private to release my pent-up grief. By the end of my time in New York City, though, I found occasional joy, seeing life in that great city persevere. But aside from the pride I gained from knowing I played even the tiniest of roles, I realized how much I cared for the work I was doing.

I found this opportunity to fulfill a purpose to be deeply rewarding. It was a chance to set out and achieve something. In the beginning I wasn't looking to be a leader; I could barely muster my own strength. I wanted to make a difference, but I came to understand that my ability to be effective was dependent on my learning leadership skills. My journey on the leadership path began at that moment. Several years later, I started capturing my thoughts on paper. This book did not end up a typical narrative, but there *is* a story—it is one of opportunity lost or gained. Failure often times begins with a lack of competence. A skillful leader, however, is better afforded a chance to achieve influence and success.

Acknowledgements

Several individuals made this book possible, including Sam Sellers, with his incredible illustrations. I thank him for his professional attitude and his dedicated workmanship throughout this project. I thank John Doolittle and Karen Cohen for their editorial reviews. *The Young Leader* would certainly be worse off in terms of substance and quality without their assistance. Thanks also to Jodie Greenberg and Alison Zeno for their input and support.

This book shares my thoughts and experience from my ongoing leadership journey and has been written over a more than five year period. It is a journal of sorts and not a research project. However, that is not to say that I haven't been influenced by many, including some whose names and works have faded from my memory, though the inspiration they created in me remains. In appreciation of those whose names and works I can recall, and who directly and indirectly, formally and informally made my growth possible, I'd like to acknowledge their instruction, wisdom, and mentorship.

Thank you to: David Castanon, Lt. Gen. (Ret.) Robert L. Van Antwerp, Jr., Lt. Gen. (Ret.) Robert B. Flowers, Brig. Gen. Mark Toy, Col. (Ret.) Thomas H. Magness, IV, Col. Kimberly M. Colloton, Brian Moore, David Boals, Carol Miller, Maureen Webster, Lt. Col. Steve Sigloch, Staff at the Army Management Staff College, Scott Elbin, Jim Collins and his *Good to Great*, Tom Fox and his Federal Coach Blog, Tom Rath and his *StrengthsFinders 2.0*, Paul Hersey and Ken Blanchard with their Situational Leadership®Model, Robert Bolton and Dorothy Grover Bolton with their *Peoples Styles at Work*, and Junior Achievement USA.

Part I. Why This Book Needs to Be Different

I'm young. I want to make a difference and lead. At first, I didn't know where to start.

At its core, the study of leadership is about the art of influencing others to achieve an end, a mission. That end can be anything, but it most often reflects a result that is different and better—and that is why the art of leadership and a desire for change coexist so neatly. Change is the mechanism that many, especially in our generation, cling to in the hope of contributing in some small way towards re-imagining our world. This desire to act transcends idealism; it is a serious reflection on the breadth of society's challenges and the sober realization that there is much hard work to be done.

When we talk about leadership, it is common to throw around expressions like "he's a leader" or "that organization lacks direction." Our shared vocabulary and our shared understanding of leadership, however, doesn't seem sophisticated enough to encompass how good leaders develop and their potential—day to day—to bring about positive, transformational change to an organization. This deprives us of a constructive dialogue that is focused and forward-looking.

I don't think it is hyperbole to say that leadership (or lack thereof) is a driving force behind everything we have become and everything we will be. Instinctively, we understand who leaders are and what they should do. They provide direction. They impact people. They produce success or failure. Regarding leadership at those macro levels, however, says nothing about its profundity, which is so all-encompassing it is nearly impossible to consider the various moving parts—let alone understand how they work together towards accomplishing change.

Our inarticulateness may also contribute to an inability to humanize the leaders we seek. In my experience, when called upon to name "a favorite leader," people's answers are often limited, including citations to the cannon of dead, white men (for example, Lincoln, John F. Kennedy, Jesus). That's fine, but certainly there must be more. And indeed, when one asks "who inspires you?", the responses become more thoughtful and varied. Inspiration, which is a cornerstone of the influence required to be a leader, is just more accessible, more real than describing someone as a leader.

After years of study and teaching, as well as the experience I gained as a young civilian leader in the Army—an organization whose mission is synonymous with leadership development—I have found we frequently ascribe unattainable characteristics to our leaders. Since our shared notion of what comprises leadership is so vague, or at least ill-defined, we also tend to think of our leaders in the abstract. Despite this, and whether or not we think our leaders can succeed, our expectations of them personally and professionally are lofty: unassailable performance, impeccable pedigree, harrowing courage, and maybe even an aesthetic ideal. These standards certainly rule out most anyone who would willingly walk the path of leadership.

Grasping the enormity of the problems facing our communities, our country, and our world, our challenge is to topple the pyramid that places one distant, idealized leader on the shoulders of millions. Instead, we need millions of leaders standing shoulder to shoulder.

The premise of this book, and the key to harnessing ambition and guiding growth for young or emerging leaders, is to recognize:

- Those skills important to leadership success are varied but accessible for those who are motivated to take on the challenge.
- With an understanding of those key skills, there are no inherent barriers to becoming a good leader. Be that person.
- The art of leadership involves developing one's talents and layering-in skills over time.

Keep these points in mind as we further explore what makes a young leader, a good leader.

In order to open up a dialogue concerning who leads, we should also take the opportunity to explore a little deeper as to why, and especially how they lead.

For many who deliberately seek it, there is a certain moral imperative in the quest. To do it right, leadership takes time—years of development and practice. There is difficulty in navigating the task of teaming with and managing people—we're complicated, emotional, and not always reasonable. That is not to say there aren't benefits to being a leader, but most of those I've helped develop sought the challenge out of personal conviction and not for prestige or money.

To be sure, some bad people are born or become leaders... and despite good intentions, some good people are just bad leaders. I'm not so concerned with the struggle to define whether and to what extent leaders are born or made. It's a fascinating, but academic, topic. All leaders can be further developed, and I am preoccupied with the need for more people, especially our younger generation, to learn to become better leaders—and that they do so in every type of field.

There is a lot of work to be done—in business, in civil society, in government. We need to groom, develop, promote and trust those who are following their moral compass to execute a mission that benefits their chosen field.

Many organizations select individuals for leadership positions through a somewhat methodical rise through the ranks. It can be formulaic at times—to get ahead you check a series of boxes that more or less qualify you. The notion of leadership development itself can be hierarchal, often reserved as a privilege. Advancing up rigid stovepipes and through an exclusive boys club, however, reflects an outdated mentality, a one-size-fits-all attitude towards leader development and promotion.

Leadership development should be thought of as a means to broadly grow the skills of individuals, whether they are headed for the executive suite or are in the trenches, working on teams. The process is about improving upon talents and layering in skills over time through learning and experience. That's not an original idea, but it's also not one that's widely discussed, in my experience. If it were, it might make leadership seem more democratic, more attainable.

There is not one imperative talent, nor one critical skill, required to produce a good leader. There is also not one all important motto, formula, or guru that can guide you. It's difficult to rush leadership development. Those who hasten it typically take a "last-in wins" approach whereby the most recent idea a person comes across controls thought and action until the next cliché supersedes it.

Instead, layering is slower, almost respectfully hesitant. It's more deliberate, in that it should be sensitive to one's leadership needs at any given moment. Finally, the success of layering comes from developing a conscious approach to integrating knowledge and experience. This may seem intuitive, but it's not always easy.

Layers of leadership, from communication skills to strategic planning to performance management, among others, need to be acknowledged in context, understood in their most basic form, and then actively engaged as a tool or resource in leading.

What does the young leader look like?

In politics and government we need individuals who, for the public good, look long-term, actively problem solve, lack presumption and pretension, act inclusively, and dedicate themselves to explaining to us why and how we must make tough decisions. No matter on which side of the political spectrum you align yourself, I hope we can agree there is important work to be done; for example, in budget policy, international affairs, defense, education, environmental protection, and more. One example of this type of young leader is Tiffiniy Cheng, the co-founder and co-director of "Fight for the Future." Cheng focuses her innovative leadership on public policy with respect to Internet-based free speech and access, as well as government transparency.

In business and industry we need leaders who, in the pursuit of profit, also support long-term economic growth, make good community partners, and integrate environmental sustainability in their operations as well as furthering the critical interests of science, health, and technology. One such leader I've come across is Craig Hanson, a partner at Next World Capital, a venture capital and asset management firm. Among Hanson's diverse accomplishments, he has lent his business savvy to a group promoting entrepreneurship in areas of extreme poverty.

Within the fields of non-profit, academia, and religion, we need leaders who address, either directly or indirectly, the challenges of society's greatest problems. We need leaders who can re-build communities, and others who can stimulate thought and action on an individual level. There is nothing and no one these leaders cannot impact with their work. One talented person who comes to mind is David Flink, co-founder and Chief Empowerment Officer of Project Eye-to-Eye, which empowers school-age youth struggling with dyslexia.

Reflecting on leadership at this moment in time and in this way is crucial. We have immediate challenges, and we must embark on finding solutions as quickly as possible. Once we develop more and better leaders, we will need to muster patience and allow them to act.

Now, I'd like to share a few words on the origin of the book and my hopes for it.

I have faced the challenges of a young leader, and I understand what is important to those who are similarly situated as I was—with big goals, little experience, many challenges, and more than a little anxiety.

At the beginning of my journey, I resolved to undertake a thorough study of the field of leadership, but I found the body of work to be frighteningly immense. I read many books and I learned a lot, but I couldn't find a succinct source that addressed many of the basic lessons as they apply to a young, emerging leader. I wanted to know the important skills, but also how to stay sane—while succeeding and progressing. I was interested in the practical—what should the developing leader focus on...and when? Whom do I solicit for advice...and how? I needed less theory and fewer inspirational mottos. I wanted more of the practical and the relevant.

I didn't find it. Instead, I sought out and collected morsels of insight from here and there. I weighed different approaches and tested them in practice. Over time I pieced together a diverse leadership montage. Eventually, I decided to create the resource myself that I had unsuccessfully sought when starting out. I'm still on the path of learning, but I've got a fair amount of experience behind me now, and I'm eager to help others on their journey.

For me, leadership is one part of my life that creates meaning. Yes, like any professional enterprise, it's a way to put one's skills to good use, but it also brings about a very personal feeling of significance. It makes me happy. It challenges me. By influencing others, it makes me feel as though I can multiply the impact of my work.

As part of that work, which now includes teaching and mentoring, I have tried to put to rest the notion that there is a mystery to the art of leadership. Indeed, whether you are thinking about the challenges you face as an emerging leader, or you are currently in the trenches and struggling to establish your credentials on the job (as I did), the tenets of good leadership are accessible, and we can find the words to identify them.

This book aspires to challenge fellow young, emerging leaders and is focused on understanding and positioning them to develop those fundamental skills critical to success. This concept is especially crucial as we Generation X'ers and Millennials frantically chase down the institutional knowledge housed within the retiring boomer generation. The passing on of this wisdom will reflect the success or failure of our generational transition, and the challenge could become a motivating source for change and innovation.

The goal is ambitious—that is, we as young leaders can summarily improve upon and perhaps hasten our development by embracing the succinct and no-nonsense lessons contained here. And through layering, we can set a course for long-term and integrated learning, using this book as a springboard into other information-rich sources.

What follows is, I'm certain, only a small piece of the puzzle. I present a model for on-the-job individual development situated in a more or less traditional, medium-to-large, organization with a leadership level above and subordinate staff below. Although this situation won't apply to everyone, it's the basis of much of my leadership experience, and I do believe many of the lessons I've distilled from this experience are broadly applicable.

This book, then, contains fifty of my best lessons—trimmed down, bottom-lined, and organized into bite-sized morsels. Although I'm not certain I can claim to be the originator of anything new, I hope the synthesis of ideas here is compelling and the format, engaging. And while this book does discuss what it takes to get ahead, the principles can assist all those who seek leadership success, despite your career aspirations.

These lessons are also reminders to be returned to as needed, whether to prepare for a challenge, brainstorm solutions for a difficult issue, gather the strength to press on, or even provide the inspiration to move up to the next level of your career.

The book has four sections beyond this introduction. Chapter II, "I'm New," includes foundational information for those who are newer to the leadership role. Chapter III, "I'm Overwhelmed," contains sections on how to troubleshoot common leadership challenges. Chapter IV, "I'm Looking to Impress," moves the discussion to the next level, an understanding of how to begin to use what you've learned in order to enhance your career and your organization. Finally, Chapter V, "I'm Ready to Pay It Forward," brings the reader full circle, from helping yourself to helping others realize their leadership potential.

The individual lessons build upon one another but can also be read on their own. Each is several pages in length and divided into multiple components for easy review. Get started with "Happy Hour Wisdom," an introductory quip to get the lesson started on a fun note. Next, I will tell you the "Ugly Truth" of the matter at hand, compressing the challenge into its basest form. I then describe the "Bottom Line," with just enough need-to-know insight to help you understand the issue. Next, I provide suggested ways to explore, implement, or mediate the issue in a section entitled "Try This." From there, I illustrate the principles discussed with a brief personal example in a "5-Second Anecdote." If you wish, in the Appendix there is a template "Crib Sheet" that can be used to guide note-taking, connect ideas, and otherwise begin to apply what you've learned.

Progress through the book as the leadership demands of your job (or your aspirations) require. Have patience in absorbing, exploring, and applying the lessons that follow. Innovate to grow faster and better.

As you move forward in this book and in your career, remember that while some leaders may be born to the task, most leaders are made—or, more precisely, self-made. Being human, we make serious work of improving on our own innate talents, and enhancing those with developed skills. Let this force drive you. It is perfectly good and natural to expect more of oneself. A better leader is a better provider—for your organization, your people, and yourself.

Part II. I'm New

Feel Connected to Your Mission

Happy Hour Wisdom

In finding purpose, you will discover success.

The Ugly Truth
Sometimes you feel as straight as an arrow, headed in the right direction. Sometimes, it is difficult to recall why you are working so damn hard. During good days and bad, it's about more than just survival. You will be better situated to succeed if you are consciously aware of and consistently attuned to the purpose of your work. The problem is it's easier said than done.

The Bottom Line
Accomplishing one's mission is an end state; it is the ultimate goal that leaders pursue. Every organization has a mission. There may be the ever-more expansive mission creep, there may be the lack of a stated mission, or there may be an ill-defined mission. Your job is to understand the mission as best you can and to feel so deeply about fulfilling it that others come to share your beliefs and follow you.

Try This
Depending on the extent to which you are in a position to drive your organization's agenda, you may have little impact on defining the mission—and that's okay for now. You can still make a big difference in helping others see the big picture, and in doing so, you fulfill that critical leader's role: helping to shape the thoughts and actions of others.

To establish an enthusiasm for fulfilling your organization's mission, intellectually connect to and emotionally invest in it. Remember back to why you applied for your job. Why did you choose this organization or this field of work? Were you guided by a passion or an opportunity to experience something new or do something great? Consider the present. What interests you about your job? What tasks satisfy you? What challenges motivate you? Think ahead. Where can you help lead the organization? What do you personally want to accomplish? What excites you about the future here?

If you try to do so, but over time cannot connect to the mission, that's okay; it happens to many of us at some point. The next step is more complicated, however, and includes thinking seriously about moving on to a new job, a new organization, or a new career.

5-Second Anecdote

Good people are sometimes just in the wrong job. I remember being in the chain of command of a smart, energetic young employee, let's call him "Wrong Seat Will." Will took his mission very seriously. The problem was that he was not pursuing *my* mission; he acted solely in his own self-interest. He disregarded company policy, upset fellow staff members, and ended up wasting company time and money. Eventually he discovered his talent and drive could be put to better use elsewhere. Sometimes we learn as much from a "what not to do" lesson—this difficult experience is a reminder to connect back to your mission, work hard at achieving it, and make sure your enthusiasm is catching.

Be Responsible

Happy Hour Wisdom

Responsibility is a burden and an opportunity.

The Ugly Truth

It's almost too obvious to say—but something we as young leaders must carefully consider is that we are responsible for everything that happens within our organization. It is a leader's ultimate burden.

The Bottom Line

As a leader, your work needs to be much more than just a job. It's why you can't afford to just clock in and out every day. Leaders invest emotional, intellectual, and physical energy in ensuring the mission gets done the right way. We are accountable for every outcome of every component of our enterprise and for every person under our charge.

A Young Aung San Suu Kyi, Burmese Activist / Politician and Nobel Laureate

Try This

Being responsible means you possess a sphere of influence within your organization that you must understand and for which you must be prepared to answer. First, know what's happening. In fact, attempt to know more about your sphere than anyone else. Read everything: reports, briefings, data, etc., for the purpose of comprehending both the big picture and the necessary details. Regularly get out from behind your desk to talk and solicit opinions—from both staff and subordinate leaders. Ask open-ended questions. Listen with an open mind. Next, with an understanding of the organization, you are accountable for assessing its needs and implementing any actions it requires. Much of the rest of this book occupies itself with outlining what a good leader does to ensure he or she properly cares for the needs of the organization and its people. The fulfillment of this trust is the essence of upholding one's responsibility as a leader.

5-Second Anecdote

Every leader at some point transitions from a position in which they did not bear the responsibility of a leader. In my teaching, I try to talk explicitly about this transition and its consequences. I try to impart the notion that new leaders should recognize this point as a break: from a time in which accountability was limited to a time in which it is great. Your actions as a leader moving forward should adjust to this greater burden, and it is reflected in the need to keep learning and building upon one's experience. We discuss both the personal risk and opportunity in assuming such a burden—it is a choice a leader makes.

Achieve Strategic Depth

Happy Hour Wisdom

Look deeper for a higher thinking.

The Ugly Truth

You may be very smart, but you may not be thinking at the depth and with the breadth and context required of you.

The Bottom Line

Strategic thinking is a critical skill for young leaders to develop. Think of an analog clock—you know how to read it, but do you know how it works? Do you understand how the gears interact behind its face? It is this looking and thinking behind what you see that can get you to this next level. This may seem pitifully obvious, and some people intuitively do it, but others do not. This more carefully considered thought process separates good leaders from their less accomplished peers.

Try This

Begin by articulating a concern, a challenge, an incongruity, etc. Consider what you know and move outwards, thinking comprehensively about how those facts relate to the broader organization and the market within which it is situated. Carefully connect one thought to the next, and challenge yourself by asking questions and predicting an array of answers. For example: Are the relationships I've established fixed? Am I overlooking any critical information? What variables might intercede? What would the consequences be? You know you've reached an end to your efforts when you come up with something new, a novel way of thinking about the issue or a potential solution. If you're unsuccessful, set aside, but return to the concern once your head is cleared.

Strategic thinking should be differentiated from run-of-the-mill problem solving. Strategic thinking may begin with a less-than-structured problem and may end with a less-than-definitive answer. The reason is that strategic thinking is a process, a way to make connections and consider possibilities that may otherwise prove elusive. This type of thinking is both broad and deep; concerning both internal and external potentialities.

Note that strategic depth, loosely defined as a method of thinking with greater tactical implications, is contrasted with strategic planning in Part IV. Strategic planning is a more structured process, though also focused on future outcomes.

5-Second Anecdote

One of the most challenging aspects of moving from a non-leadership position upwards is to broaden one's operating picture to produce a better understanding of the moving parts that function together to drive the organization. When I hired "Anxious to Act Andy" to a top-level position, he was one of the brightest go-getters I had met—and I knew him to produce some of the best technical work products I had seen. But once promoted to leadership, and when my requests veered from the formulaic, Andy struggled. For example, I assigned him to produce a presentation for the organization's leadership on a topic with self-evident facts, but less obvious implications. In preparation, he dutifully identified relevant pieces of the story, but he didn't have a thoughtful or thought-provoking narrative. There was nothing insightful. I stepped in and coached him on some potential directions, and that was all he needed to get up and running. In hindsight, the narrative usually seems intuitive, but it's not—without practice. Creating the spark that pro-vokes a fire of strategic thought takes leader-like skill.

Do the Right Thing

Happy Hour Wisdom

Good judgment meets with good ends.

The Ugly Truth

Typical leaders like to make decisions, but they often face constraints that delay their response. For example, needing to meet legal, regulatory or certain internal process requirements can slow you down and may prove expensive. Ethical considerations can also be complicated and difficult to resolve. The issue is how to balance doing the right thing with managing risk and making a good decision. Depending on the issue, the stakes can be high. Take the challenge seriously.

The Bottom Line

Some people will ask, "Will this get the job done?" Leaders ask, "Will this get the job done *right*?" Confident decision-making comes from exploring all perspectives of a situation, and at a minimum, understanding that you need to ask good questions in order to get to the answers that justify your decision.

Try This

Do temper your reasoning with good judgment: be guided by principle even when something looks like an easy get. Filter decisions through multiple layers. Be legal—know what the law is: be aware of what lies in a gray area and what does not. Be ethical—consider what principles are important to uphold in any given circumstance. Go further and explicitly create an office environment where ethical questions are openly discussed in order to pursue the highest of standards. Know how to assess risk. Understand the difference between law, policy, and practice. If you are pushing a boundary, recognize that and be prepared to defend it.

Don't fear the complexity of some issues or become squeamish or hesitant at the prospect of resolving them. Doing the right thing requires careful thought, but not indecision. Don't fall into the trap of thinking that past practice can determine future success—things change. Don't be naïve about how you make your decisions—utilize critical thinking skills to examine your biases and assumptions. Recognize that data may be incomplete or just bad. Still others may provide poor advice or attempt to manipulate you towards a certain end.

A Young Abraham Lincoln

5-Second Anecdote

I remember early in my leadership career, I was in a position to recommend a certain course of action to a new superior. The project was a controversial one, and the choice of options was by no means clear. I went all out, however, and assured my superior that this path was the right one to follow. I ended up failing in multiple ways—first, I had not considered all the implications of my course of action (it was a little more unorthodox and risky than I truly anticipated); then, there was a moral consideration that I did not attend to (about which my customer should have been forewarned); and finally, despite the poor decision itself, the execution was flawed (I hadn't strategized the best way to involve my superior in the decision-making process—I had a "trust me" attitude). My want or need to make a decision came before I had fully vetted the consequences. In the end, looking at my proposed course of action through a legal and ethical prism may have led to the same decision, but I would have done a better job on the follow-through.

Develop an Organizational Style that Works for You

Happy Hour Wisdom

A clear vision of oneself precedes true enlightenment.

The Ugly Truth

You've probably heard the following: "Stay on top of this," "Don't let it fall through the cracks," "See this through," "Keep on it," "Don't lose sight of that," "Stick with it," etc. These are the frustrated pleas of one imploring another to be conscious of how he or she does their work. Don't let anyone doubt your abilities. Address the chaos of your organizational routine by recognizing where you can improve and creating a system that integrates the best of your personal habits and the requirements of your leadership role.

The Bottom Line

For multiple reasons, it is important to be organized and aware of how you use time—it models good behavior, creates efficiencies, and allows you to prioritize mission requirements. You may be thinking that your skills have gotten you this far—what more do you need to know about taking notes, scheduling appointments, or providing follow-up on tasks? The bottom line is that it's not entirely about learning something new—it's about seeing yourself anew and using that understanding to enhance your style.

Try This

Leadership often requires quickly and adequately processing a lot of information from multiple sources, including meeting notes, correspondence, emails, reports, personal conversations, and more. Think about where and how your information is stored and retrieved. Can you easily access needed details? Do you lose things? How responsive are you to others? How do you formulate your 'to do' list? If you need additional clarity, ask close associates which of your work habits are effective and which ones are less so.

Read up on time management—it's more of a science than you'd think. Have you tried the "one-touch" method? What about the "tickler file system." Can you set aside dedicated times to undertake key tasks (for example, creative time, organization time, reading time)? Also examine which tools—new or upgraded—might make a difference for you. Have you been avoiding purchasing or implementing new hardware or software? Do you need an old-fashioned day planner, or can you afford a personal assistant to keep you organized?

Look to the habits and skills you admire in others as a guide to what changes you could make in your own style. Enlist an organizational manager, a space planner—whatever it takes. Understand that time spent upgrading how you work will pay dividends later on. Keep an open mind and, of course, don't be afraid to change. Finally, when you do make a change, trust the set-up and stick with it.

A Young Hillary Rodham Clinton

5-Second Anecdote

Every story I have on maximizing my organizational style begins and ends the same: at some point I wake up from the routine I've lived for months or years and realize that I should have been smart enough to break free from whatever inefficiency—large or small—has held me back. One admittedly unsexy example is my personal note-taking and task-tracking system (or lack thereof). I once had a promotion that required me to up my game, but I was plagued by the inability to keep on top of my new responsibilities. I wrote notes everywhere; it took me too long to consolidate my action items; and I couldn't find what I needed in a timely manner. I finally had a heart-to-heart with myself and admitted that my constant attempts to operate within the messy paradigm I was used to weren't working. I then started to pay close attention to my actions, and I watched how others organized themselves. I found a few new apps for my tablet and eventually cajoled myself into a system that made sense for me. Best wakeup call ever.

Leave Space for a Leadership Style of Your Own

Happy Hour Wisdom

Be your own style guru.

The Ugly Truth

This book notwithstanding, leadership advice can be pervasive and perhaps even overwhelming. That can be frustrating, when figuring out what type of leader you are and how you should strive to develop, is of such critical importance.

The Bottom Line

Don't let anyone tell you who you should be. Different approaches to leadership aren't necessarily bad, and talking about style is useful in terms of distinguishing and evaluating practices. Leaders do act differently but should strive to end at the same place—influencing others to accomplish the mission.

A Young John F. Kennedy

Try This

Each leader is ultimately responsible for the magnitude of his or her own development, including a consideration of those elements of style that reflect our individuality.

Also recognize that we mature as leaders over time. Pace your development by mentally balancing what you are learning with your comfort level and skill need at any given time. This will help ensure changes in your style are subtle, deliberate, and sustainable.

As to individual style, be cautious to not over-moderate yourself in order to avoid standing out. Respect your own strengths and instincts and seek to develop a healthy representation of who you are and what your position requires of you.

As you determine what type of leader you are and how you may develop, focus precisely. Understand leadership differences based on substance (the knowledge and practice integral to doing your job) and style (the manner in which you do your job). Substantive deficiencies in the former can be mitigated by working hard and seeking additional mentorship or training. Correction of the latter may be needed if it is interfering with the accomplishment of your job and can be corrected by consultation with close peers, through various leadership development classes or tools, or even with the aid of outside coaches.

Finally, in the daunting days at the beginning of my leadership journey, I had to deliberately remember to cut myself some slack from time to time. If you find yourself similarly situated, recall that you were hired or promoted for a reason; you got where you are by possessing some measure of talent or skill. Besides, different types of leaders (those with various strengths) are needed in different jobs at different times. Respect what you bring to the table and don't try to be someone you are not. It's usually not possible, and it's certainly not desirable.

Five Second Anecdote

At the beginning of my leadership journey I didn't feel as though I belonged at the big boy/girl conference table. I looked like them (button-down shirt, tie, dress pants, wingtips), but I didn't feel like I was one of them. I was younger, more willing to think differently, and more apt to innovate. I earned my place at the table, but I felt the need to distinguish myself. So I rolled up my shirt sleeves and got to work.

Literally, that was it. I rolled up my sleeves and have kept them that way ever since. Whether hot or cold, I kept them rolled—ready to pounce on the next challenge to come my way. It was a small stylistic flourish; I was usually the only one at executive meetings without neatly pressed and buttoned sleeves. People may not have noticed, I don't know. It was only for the benefit of my own self-confidence, a reminder that I didn't mind feeling set apart, an emerging leader with a style of his own.

Find a Mentor and a Sponsor

Happy Hour Wisdom

Seek out the wise; they've been down these paths before.

The Ugly Truth

Earlier in life, I often chafed at the notion of having a mentor. It just seemed so, well, affected. In truth, as you attempt to differentiate yourself as a leader, the trajectory of your learning must be exponential, and an effective mentor relationship can help you get to that place faster. Without it, your work will be that much more difficult.

A Young Plato

The Bottom Line

The mentor/mentee relationship can be a safe place to discuss your professional challenges and opportunities. A mentor is not your competition, not your evaluator, not someone who will be angry or disappointed in you. A mentor can be a sounding board, a source of expertise, and a friendly ear. The key is that you have a lot of responsibility as a leader, and you do not have to bear it alone.

Most people have heard about the concept of "mentor," but fewer have considered a sponsor, an idea that has become more prominent in recent years. As it goes, while a mentor works with you more intensely on professional development, a sponsor works with you explicitly on professional advancement. A sponsor is positioned to promote you to others; for example, encouraging you for greater assignments and maybe even promotions.

Try This

A mentor or sponsor doesn't just fall into your lap. It takes some consideration to weigh who has the skills to provide you with thoughtful, appropriate advice or who is in a position to guide your future success. Seek input from people you respect. Don't be afraid to consider someone unconventional or considerably beyond your pay grade. Maybe this person doesn't even know you well...yet.

When you find that right person, meet regularly. Plan ahead to make the best use of your time together. Typically, mentor relationships are improvement-based; for example reading and discussing subjects related to professional growth or providing constructive feedback on problems or weaknesses. Sponsor relationships are based more on developing networks or career insights. Think deeply about what you would like to accomplish and go from there. When it's time to meet, lose the modesty and check your inhibitions at the door—discuss your strengths and challenges, how you feel about your career and where you would like it to go, etc. Respect your mentor/sponsor—keep the relationship professional and ask for nothing more than his or her time. And when they promote you to others—don't disappoint.

5-Second Anecdote

As a young, emerging leader, I wanted to develop a mentor relationship to grow my understanding of the organization from the inside out. So I went straight to the top, and I humbly asked the number two person in charge (let's call him "Runs It All Paul") to be my mentor. I had to work twice as hard to make our sessions productive—I did not want to be seen as just an opportunistic hanger-on. Indeed, I took full responsibility for our meetings—including when, where, and what would be discussed—because Paul was too busy to do more than just sit there and be brilliant. I learned from him about strategic decision-making, how the organization was structured, and why command and control was set up as such—insights that were invaluable in my effort to deconstruct and understand other programs and further key relationships. In the twilight of his mature career, our sessions also served as an opportunity for Paul to pass on his knowledge to the next generation; a win-win-win for him, me, and the organization.

Be/Play Nice

Happy Hour Wisdom

Investing well in others will pay dividends.

The Ugly Truth

Gamesmanship infuses many areas of our lives. Jockeying, positioning, and game-playing are natural embodiments of the struggle to win in the office as well. They do not, however, represent an ideal state. If we turn away from the possibility of empathy, generosity, and kindness, we lose sight of the best of ourselves, and maybe even a leadership opportunity.

The Bottom Line

This is one of those I-learned-it-in-kindergarten lessons. If you want others to treat you well and treat you fair—respond in kind.

A Young Cesar Chavez

Try This

Use personality type assessment tools and conflict styles inventories to understand why people act and react in certain ways and calibrate your interaction accordingly. Look for ways to understand and fulfill people's interests, what they really want, and not the positions they've staked.

See the best in people, and otherwise hear their points of view before drawing conclusions. Use strategy to outsmart or outmaneuver difficult office players. Remain calm and constructive, even amidst the pettiness, bickering, labeling, and dishonesty that characterize some who prefer to "play dirty. " When the going gets bad, defend yourself, certainly, but know that ill-acting, angry or impatient individuals often seal their own fate. Sometimes all you need to do is take the high road—not the bait.

5-Second Anecdote

I once knew a supervisor, let's call him "By the Rule Riley." Riley was a tough supervisor. His relentless desire for things to be accomplished in a prescribed manner was hard on staff. Many became alienated or burned out. Riley had his own brand of leadership, and it was certainly not always healthy. His example serves to remind me of how far removed we as leaders can become from rank and file staff. Our actions are magnified a hundred fold in their eyes because they so rely on our care (feedback, praise, support) for quality of work, life, and development. What Riley needed to do was balance his strong hand with a kinder touch, looking for ways to be magnanimous, when appropriate. These actions would have allowed him to preserve his style, which did yield results, but also infuse some empathy to engender more employee satisfaction and greater respect. That's the best rule, in my opinion.

Make a Personal Connection

Happy Hour Wisdom

Take the time to care for others.

The Ugly Truth

In case you haven't figured it out yet—leadership isn't always fun. It's hard work, there's lots of responsibility, and sometimes, there are trouble makers. Staff may talk about you or even plot against you (behind or in front of your back)—and your desire for basic mutual respect may be just wishful thinking. Still, it's up to you to strategize how to take on naysayers and improve or maintain positive staff morale.

A Young Phil Jackson

The Bottom Line

Most staff are great, and just want to engage their leader on a deeper level. Other staff, however, may act out in ways that are counter-productive. But in doing so, consider that they are sending you a message. Many just want to be heard. This doesn't mean you need to indulge every request. You can, however, make a personal connection that attempts to bridge a challenging working environment.

Try This

Learn the lesson of being a situational leader. Each member of your team has different needs and will respond optimally to varying leadership styles. Attempt to understand at all costs who your staff is and what they need. Once you do that, provide them attention—that alone goes a long way in improving their happiness. If you're not a natural "people person," make a concerted effort to develop your "soft skills." Communicate properly (see "Understand What It Means to Communicate" later in this part). Dedicate yourself to providing a friendly working environment. Finally, spend quality time: go to your office happy hour, host a lunchtime pot-luck, engage your staff in lively competitions and team-building events.

One note of caution: developing a personal connection does not resolve the challenge of a malcontent who is also a poor performer. It sends a bad signal to high performers when poor performers appear to be coddled. It takes balance, but performance management (the setting, counseling, and ensuring achievement of performance objectives) and caring for individuals are not mutually exclusive.

5-Second Anecdote

I have a story of an employee, let's call her "Luv Me First Linda." Linda is great in so many ways—technically proficient in her work, customer-friendly, and a pleasure to have in the office. I made a mistake when she first came to my unit, however, by assuming she would respond to my leadership style in the same way as my other staff. Linda was different; she was turned off by my direct approach to providing feedback, including constructive criticism. I learned through trial and error that I needed to couch my feedback for her in a less direct way and with plenty of positive reinforcement. In doing so I found I could engage Linda in any performance-related discussion. See, I do luv ya, Linda!

Have Patience; Be Even-Tempered

Happy Hour Wisdom

Silence is sometimes the wisest response.

The Ugly Truth

The self-control required to tolerate delay and maintain composure are among the more difficult of the leadership lessons presented in this book.

The Bottom Line

The need for patience, and with it a balanced approach to decision-making, is one of the biggest lessons I've learned in my relatively young career. The process of re-orienting the pace at which you listen and engage others may seem artificial. And for many, especially us younger leaders, it's not easy. At first, I thought I was betraying my leader-like instincts to act quickly and decisively. With more experience, however, I found the additional time given to interact and reflect put other, more subtle and insightful, aspects of decision-making into play.

Try This

Before you respond to a given matter, take a deep breath. During that breath, take the time to look at the problem/issue from all angles. The more likely you are to exhibit a strong emotion—anger, shaming, etc.—the longer you should take to weigh and control your response. Ask yourself whether you have listened carefully enough to others. Consider whether your understanding of the situation would be aided by additional inquiry. Ensure you've brought critical thinking skills to bear on your reasoning (See "Keep Critical Distance" in Part III). As you work through your thought process internally, on the exterior you should appear calm. Heightened emotion displayed at the right time and in the right way may sometimes produce intended results—just play that card consciously and sparingly.

Note that fast and appropriate decision-making responses can go hand in hand (and indeed sometimes an immediate response is necessary), but this skill is most prominent in well-developed and experienced leaders. As we young leaders train ourselves to think and act deliberately under pressure, we too will reduce our response time.

5-Second Anecdote

Overall, I'm typically calmer than most, but I'm also prone to occasional acts of melodrama. I remember having numerous meetings with a subordinate supervisor (let's call her "Quick to Temper Tanya"). Tanya was hot-blooded, eager to battle, constantly jockeying, and bent on manipulating a given situation to her terms. I restrained my dialogue with her because the one thing she found difficult to overcome was sickeningly deliberate and grossly unemotive logic. The ability to remain personally in control of myself, unfazed either by another's antics or a challenging problem, usually gave me the upper hand. In truth, I was striving to act beyond an instinct to play into the histrionics, and in doing so, outmaneuver a difficult office player.

Find Your Inner Investigative Reporter

Happy Hour Wisdom

The question asked is as important as an answer given.

The Ugly Truth

There is no place for passivity in leadership. If you refrain from diving right into the work that needs to get done, you're finished. Don't know where to start? For those who are new to leadership, new to a company, new to an issue, or if you just plain want to understand what's happening around the organization, you should have lots of questions, and you can't be timid in asking them.

The Bottom Line

Good leaders seek the truth, not what they want to or expect to hear. If your concern for the mission is genuine, a sincere curiosity should follow. Just be certain to seek out good sources for your good questions.

A Young Lisa Ling

Try This

Play the journalist to seek out truth. Journalists rely on good sense to seek facts and piece together helpful narratives. You should ask open-ended, thoughtful questions of subordinates as well as peers. Once you've started posing the good questions, remember to remain open to different facts, opinions, and perspectives. Seek out understated or overlooked nuggets of truth and inspiration. Encourage yourself to have enough sense and self-confidence to incorporate the good advice of others, or even altogether cede ground to a superior course of action. If you suspect that you are anything less than completely open to counsel, you must take this on as an urgent personal challenge.

5-Second Anecdote

I have come to understand that some leadership lessons can be learned by accessing and integrating other, often disparate, elements of one's own education and experience. For me, I did a fair share of university coursework in journalism. I am, therefore, less predisposed to write an end to a story before gathering as much information as possible. This means doing legwork (research, question, research, question, and so on) and being open to where the inquiry leads. To be sure, this pits my journalist's drive for the truth against my leader's urge to be decisive. I have nicknamed myself in this internal battle as "Veritas Victor," and whenever I am in a position to referee an issue and render a decision, I attempt to overcome instinct and let the truth-seeking process play out.

Understand What It Means to Communicate

Happy Hour Wisdom

Speaking or writing is easy; saying something takes effort.

The Ugly Truth

If you don't have well-developed communication skills, you have little chance of being a good leader. If you don't have an organization that communicates efficiently and effectively, there is little hope for mission success.

The Bottom Line

Communication is one of the most fundamental characteristics that defines an organization. Words (or a lack thereof) are powerful—even as young leaders we understand this. The challenge lies in understanding and optimizing communications—between staff, among teams, up and down the ladder, and even outside the organization.

Try This

Communication is more than just getting words across; it is using those words to create for another person the right meaning at the right time. It's not perfection; it's judgment combined with skill. This advice applies on both the individual and the organizational levels.

Good communication doesn't happen by accident—it takes planning and practice. Effective communications are consistent; they indicate direction, but they also reflect the organization and the individual's core values and culture (see "Understand Organizational Culture..." in Part IV). When you speak or write, do so deliberately: control your message and calibrate your emotion (whether restrained, impassioned, or even forceful).

Achieving the right amount and type of communications is a key to success. Seek a good balance; understanding that too much is inundating and too little is frustrating. When in possession of a particular piece of information, either developed by or passed on to you, I was taught to ask the question "Who else needs to know what I know?" Then take appropriate action to ensure it gets passed on.

Beyond this, leaders have the responsibility to understand their organization's needs and initiate appropriate communications to proactively direct work, explain policies, deliver news, etc. Largely reactive communications indicate a lack of strategy in communications planning. The good news is that most organizations understand and place great value on getting communications right, and they have created a multitude of teams to see to it (possibly including: community/external relations/outreach, public relations, public affairs, marketing, even human resources). Seek out your experts and/or outside resources to help craft and deliver your message. Just remember that we as leaders are ultimately responsible for the effort's success or failure.

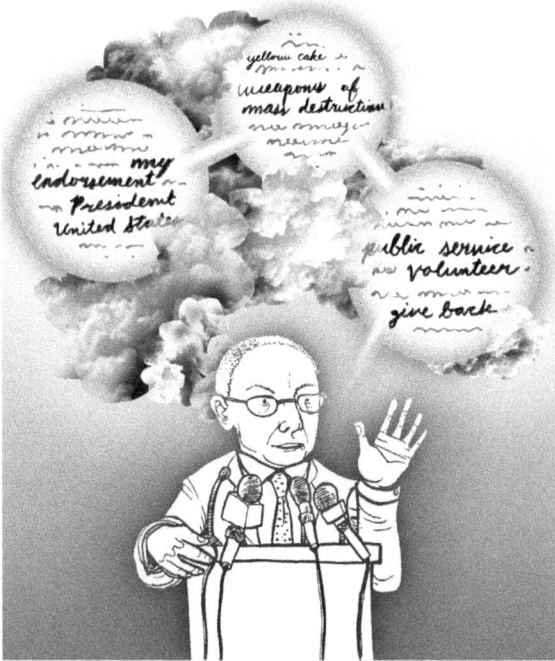

A Young Colin Powell

5-Second Anecdote

The biggest difference between a good leader and a great leader is the ability to communicate effectively. I'm thinking about two subordinate leaders I have mentored, let's call them "Quik 2 Judge Quinn" and "Slow & Sure Sam"—both of them of similar age, resume, and technical talent. I really like Quinn, and I know someday she's going to be a great leader, but right now she has difficulty expressing herself in the proper way and at the right time. She produces communications to staff that appear abrupt (without context) and sometimes driven by frustration. Sam is better in some ways: he is patient, careful in choosing when and how to communicate, and he has an abundance of empathy. Sam uses communication as a tool to engender shared understanding and to team-build. Quinn's communications sometimes confuse and often defeat her best efforts to build consensus and morale. Guess whose team I'd rather be on?

Admit Mistakes

Happy Hour Wisdom

Saying "I'm wrong" can set things right.

The Ugly Truth

Admitting when you're wrong or sorry is never fun or easy, but when you're at the top, people are looking to you to do what's right. So, you must set the example, like it or not.

A Young Jim Bakker

The Bottom Line

We are young, emerging leaders on an often treacherous learning curve—addressing ever greater issues of increasing importance. Despite the challenges, don't forget to use every opportunity to display your graciousness and class.

Saying "I was wrong" when you chose an incorrect course of action, or "I'm sorry" when you made a personal affront can show your flexibility, humanity, and comfort with yourself. It is an opportunity you may not frequently have (fortunately) to build a humble, real persona.

Try This

Let's not be dramatic here, but just rip the band-aid off already. If you did wrong, say so and move on with the air cleared. Do it in a way that is commensurate with the harm. If it was a wrong decision, cop to it. If it was a person-to-person faux pas, make a private concession. Don't make light, but use humor, if appropriate.

Take note that if you appear too frequently sorry, others may doubt your competence. If you are truly doing things wrong that often, take a more structural look at the problem and seek appropriate training or counseling.

Oh, and don't confuse actual error with insecurity. Sometimes we feel vulnerable for whatever reason or preoccupied with a risk we've taken or a position we've staked. Leaders make decisions and take risks; sometimes we're right, and sometimes we're wrong. Don't jump the gun and reach for an apology when you're feeling insecure. Straighten your back, hold your head up, and wait until the dust settles.

5-Second Anecdote

Consider a peer of mine, a very affable leader, let's call him "Nervous Neil." In answering questions about a project or the work of a subordinate, Neil will offer an apology with his response ("I'm sorry I didn't call you sooner with that information, but the project deadline is May 1st"). I know he's doing it unconsciously, and I suspect this genuflection makes him feel as though he is demonstrating concern for the recipient's inquiry; however, it only makes him look weak. This seems contradictory—this section is about learning to say "I'm wrong" or "I'm sorry"—but, alas, the key here is not to say it more often...the point is to know when to say it. Neil should remember that everyone fails to do something at some point, and before saying those magical words, he should think about whether there is a reasonable expectation for personal accountability. Sorry to say so, Neil!

Part III.   I'm Overwhelmed

Leaders Are Responsible for Their Own Morale

Happy Hour Wisdom

Only you can best take care of you.

The Ugly Truth

Leaders, just as anyone, are subject to emotional swings—from the forlorn to the ecstatic. Most young leaders, under strain to prove themselves fast, are especially vulnerable to pressure, bouts of anxiety, and maybe even depression. Regardless of the stress, however, you must be driven from within and be responsible for keeping yourself moving forward, despite setbacks or down days.

The Bottom Line

We spend most waking hours in the company of those with whom we work, and during tough times, it may seem natural to find solace or commiseration with them. Regardless, it is difficult to keep strongly-felt emotions inside. As a leader, however, it is important to insulate staff from your mood swings. In the office, remain even-tempered and as upbeat as possible, even if it's just for the sake of presentation. Leaders hold the organization together, and people look to them for confidence and self-control.

Try This

When you hit some emotional turbulence, rely on those in your personal life with whom you share a confidence—family, friends, and spiritual leaders. There's no substitute for that love and support. Share openly with them and allow them to counsel you.

It is also helpful to develop a close relationship with one or two other workplace leaders whom you can trust to exchange unfettered thoughts or an occasional emotional tirade…all in confidence and out of earshot of staff. Unlike friends and family, workplace confidants often understand the dynamics that produce work-related stress, and this can be beneficial in talking through problems.

Work stress is inevitable, of course, but must be managed. Everyone has a breaking point. Be on the lookout for warning signs of a chronic problem: chest pains, trouble sleeping, irritability or prolonged depression. See a doctor if necessary. And at the risk of preaching a little, remember the basics: eat well, exercise, and get plenty of sleep. No drugs, excessive alcohol, or other addictive behavior. If you develop a problem along these lines, it is important to seek professional help immediately.

Finally, for those times when you are simply a little 'blue', try to stay positive and keep moving forward with your life's routine, as tough times do eventually pass. Take care of you for the sake of you, for those who love you, and for your organization.

A Young Martha Stewart

5-Second Anecdote

Down days at the office can be difficult to cope with—many leaders don't recognize the extent to which satisfaction in their ability to accomplish the mission can be offset with feelings of stress caused by overwork, failure, etc. Additionally, leaders are used to having a measure of control in their lives and are disproportionately affected by an inability to steer outcomes their way.

I was faced with an important staffing issue that, no matter how hard I worked at it, I couldn't get done successfully. I knew it was the right thing to do, but the people and rules standing in my way were immovable. The pressure left me short of breath. My mind was spinning; I was obsessed with failure. I finally came to the realization that the only thing left for me to do was detach myself from the matter.

I tried to relax and take some time to think. Eventually, I decided to make one more go of it. I reconsidered the goal, restructured my efforts, readjusted my expectations, and reframed success to others. It didn't work, and I moved on. But the ability to slow my inner turmoil and regulate my emotions proved a helpful way to stop a very unproductive cycle of frustration and self-pity. It also allowed me to look for other avenues of action. The lesson was a harsh one, but I think it made me stronger in the long run.

Lean on Others' Expertise and Build Your Bench

Happy Hour Wisdom

A strong bench supports you when and where you are most weak.

The Ugly Truth

Some leaders say or think the following: *I'd feel better doing the work myself...I can get it done faster...It would take too much time to explain to someone else, and I would have to review the final product anyway...I know just how I want it done...It's just easier this way.*

It may be more common than many hands-on leaders care to admit; however, an overdependence on oneself to do routine tasks will lead to overwork, stress, and/or mission failure at some point. As difficult as it is to loosen control, do so for the long-term health of the organization and for your own sanity.

The Bottom Line

Are you attending every meeting? Do you track and follow up on all tasks large and small? Would you describe yourself as being "thorough" or "hands-on?" What your parents told you all along is true: it's not a bad thing to ask for help. As a leader, though, you need to do more than just request an occasional hand. Delegate tasks as a means of freeing your time for more strategic, leader-like work, while using the opportunity to teach and challenge your staff.

Try This

Be honest with yourself regarding the challenges of leadership—including a lack of time to directly manage certain aspects of the organization, your own knowledge gaps, and the need to empower others while keeping an eye on the important things. Seek opportunities to develop a strong and trusting cadre of people whom you can rely on to help run and manage the organization. Don't blindly trust, however—develop processes to ensure proper supervision. Ask tough questions, and follow up to make certain your expectations are being met.

Truly enable staff by sharing information and giving them the tools to succeed. These actions develop the capacity of your staff, grow expertise, build teams, and contribute to succession planning. The backing-up of skill sets also creates opportunities to handle occasional workload or workforce imbalances across your organization.

A Young Barack Obama

5-Second Anecdote

Now, I'm a pretty self-confident person, but when I was first hired into a leadership position, I was haunted by the notion that they picked the wrong guy. I was humbled by the talent of those I interviewed along-side. My insecurity led to some turf building on my part as I sought to lay claim to my duties and prove my worth. But once I waded further into the job, I did come to understand why I was there. It's the same reason why anyone is hired; my particular combination of strengths was what the organization needed. Everyone has their unique role to play. With this realization, the need to be defensive receded, and I saw myself as not just a leader, but as part of a team—a very talented team that could help me get the job done.

Claim/Reclaim Your Passion

Happy Hour Wisdom

If you lose drive, you won't get anywhere.

The Ugly Truth

To continue the metaphor, as they develop, sometimes young leaders lift their foot off the accelerator and move less energetically in the direction of achieving mission success. This can happen for a variety of reasons, not all of which are bad, but if it happens for any length of time it may breed complacency.

A Young Elon Musk

The Bottom Line

The motivation to lead often begins with a strong desire to achieve something or prove success. Over time, leaders tend to lose connection with the original emotion that ignited their purpose. This can be problematic if your intensity to accomplish the mission wanes. Satisfaction replaces passion. Plateaus in accomplishment are mistaken for summits of achievement. In the long run, a bit of self-reflection can sustain your vigilance and your performance, and keep you moving forward professionally.

Try This

To begin, consider previous leadership lessons learned. These are developmental outposts, key markers showing how far you've come in your professional growth. Trace what you learned from whom, key struggles, and memorable successes. Connect what you did to why you were doing it. Go even further back and re-examine what led you to your profession and your job in a position of responsibility. All this deliberate thought is an effort to help you understand what gave you purpose and to remind you of the path you are on. Hopefully that core excitement remains, waiting to be rediscovered. From there, strategize new ways for your enthusiasm to propel you to the next level of achievement (see Part IV "I'm Looking to Impress"). If little excitement remains, or if the downsides of the job perpetually outweigh the upsides, seriously examine whether your current position still fits you.

5-Second Anecdote

I became acquainted with one of my organization's board members, let's call him "Fire in the Hole Joel." Joel was a bit rough around the edges, emotional at times, but by all appearances enthusiastic about accomplishing the mission. He might not fit in at a lace tablecloth tea party, but I'd want him by my side at a senior-level meeting. Joel rose to leadership from the trenches—he began his career outside the headquarters office and has seen every side of our operation. Several of his children, talented in their own right, worked their way into other parts of the organization. From the outside, I can't see what motivates Joel. From our talks, though, it's evident to me that his history with and connectedness to the organization make him sensitive to the impact of leadership decisions and provide a powerful wellspring of creativity and motivation. Joel seems to have his passion figured out—and he's driving on.

Be Wary of Conformity;
Keep/Maintain Sense of Self

Happy Hour Wisdom

You are the decisions you make.

The Ugly Truth
In climbing the ladder, you've co-opted, adopted, and otherwise taken what looks good and made it work for you. That's fine; that's learning. It's also possible that when you've brought in the new, you've subjugated the old. In doing so, you may be neglecting some natural aptitude—qualities that define you and strengths or personality differences that can distinguish you from your peers.

The Bottom Line
It's time to check back in with your authentic self. Too heavy on the self-help for you? The bottom line here is not a personal or psychological reversion. I suggest that as young leaders we all possess—and need to make use of—the entirety of our strengths, from those most obvious, to those lesser-known or dormant talents or skills that could supplement or bolster the pursuit of success.

Try This
Thinking about and understanding the distinction between who you are or what you know as a result of your life's experience, formal education, culture, etc., and those layers you then add as a result of your need to develop as a leader can help remind you of your original and special aptitudes. Those added layers (strategy, communications, mentoring, etc.) are good and necessary, but all aspiring leaders are attempting to add the same ones! Look for what makes you unconventional, and perhaps more valuable.

Take pride in being you, in being the type of unique leader you are. Emphasize your natural ability—no matter how small. Sports enthusiast? I bet you have some great metaphors and are a master of cheering on the team. Person of faith? You probably have a deeper appreciation for people's holistic needs—that's a great foundation for empathy.

Movie aficionado? That can make for some great water cooler banter and bonding with staff.

A Young Richard Feynan, Chemist and Nobel Laureate

5-Second Anecdote

I have a subordinate supervisor; let's call her "Right Choice Rita," who approached me for advice regarding the need to discipline one of her staff. The conduct policy manual, which also dictates punitive measures, indicated Rita should issue the employee a lengthy suspension without pay. Rita is a parent, a nurturer, someone who naturally understands the needs of others. Her gut told her the punishment was excessive, and she made the decision to challenge a by-the-book reading of the situation. I worked with Rita to dig into the policies and explore the flexibility we as managers possess to implement them. We discussed what method of counseling would work for this particular employee, and ultimately she did implement a more lenient resolution. In general Rita doesn't flaunt her empathy, and no one would claim she's soft. I'm not certain if she even consciously acknowledged the context of her decision, but Rita's use of what she does well to get the job done right is a testament to the trust she places in her strengths.

Mercilessly Mimic Whatever Works

Happy Hour Wisdom

Enlightenment begins with understanding you do not need to have all the answers.

The Ugly Truth

When the success of an organization is at stake, there should be no pride of ownership. And while creativity is a great quality, sometimes the solutions to challenges just need to be recycled, reused or re-imagined. Don't waste time in mulling your options. If the best course of action available has already been done, copy what works.

The Bottom Line

You're on top now—you don't need to be stunning through-and-through. If it works, use it. Leaders do what it takes to accomplish the mission. Prove yourself by being effective.

A Young Franklin Roosevelt

Try This

Of course it is critical to achieve means and ends that are legal, ethical, acceptable in the public eye, capable of being done, and good for the bottom line. But within these constraints, if you can find an efficient solution—use it, regardless of its provenance. Think about or aggressively seek out what you or others have done in similar situations in the past—inside and outside your organization. If you're new, you'll need to ask questions like "Have we confronted this before?", "What did we do?", and "Did it work?" These are admittedly simple, but young leaders tend to jump right into brainstorming solutions without considering what's come before, including the lessons that have been learned. More problem-solving tips can be found in "Fake It, Then Make It," later in this part.

5-Second Anecdote

I'm always looking for new or different ways to infuse energy into my work, and sometimes ideas can be found in the least expected places. Even senior leaders whom I generally do not consider to be ideal role models often possess nuggets of wise action and survival skills gained over years of experience. I am thinking about one particular leader, let's call him "Shoot from the Hip Kip." Kip is an interesting fellow, a lumbering, self-deprecating man given to sudden, slightly grumpy interjections or outbursts at meetings. He has a penchant for saying whatever comes into his mind. Despite this, I have come to admire his honest, straight-forward attitude (and if nothing else, his consistency); these are important but often overlooked hallmarks of good leadership. I've integrated some of his more effective, less brusque, meeting techniques as a way of ensuring I am directly and honestly addressing key issues with staff, as opposed to talking around problems and issues. I mimicked Kip this once, but I'll deny it if you tell anyone.

Set Expectations

Happy Hour Wisdom

Ask for what you want.

The Ugly Truth

Unmet expectations are the primary scourge of any organization. They can lead to mistrust, performance management issues, and, possibly, failure.

A Young Martin Scorsese

The Bottom Line

The setting and fulfilling of mutual expectations goes both ways between staff and leadership. From the leader's perspective, there is a whole host of supervisory skills needed to ensure proper performance management. The foremost among these is the establishment of objectives or goals to guide what employees do and how they do it. From the staffs' perspective, the employer also makes certain job-related commitments as to what defines success, and these must be upheld in order to ensure their trust.

Try This

Setting expectations is not complicated, but it does take time and consistent effort. Annual or semi-annual performance cycles marked by frequent counseling sessions are a must. Objectives should be mutually discussed, clearly understood, and ultimately written down. Measurable goals are optimal, though there are certainly subjective aspects of performance review that are also important. When performance evaluations are made, they should be fair. As well, the evaluation of a closing cycle should be clearly defined from the new, goal-setting process of the next.

Aside from formal performance reviews, the setting of expectations can occur on a task by task basis. It's usually good to take a few extra minutes on the front end of assigning a task to describe precisely what you want done (typically answering "what," "when," and "how" questions). At times the amount of detail you can relay will differ. The key is to impart what you know. Also, it's always good to seek and consider input from staff; be careful, however, to maintain oversight of and responsibility for the process. Finally, leaders should encourage employees to ask well-considered questions throughout, and provide interim status updates or product reviews as you consider appropriate.

Conveying well what you want done is key to obtaining the work product you desire. If not, staff may make assumptions, and with that, you'll have no cause for complaint if your vision isn't met. If you have laid out clear expectations, that's great ... just don't forget to follow-up on the requirements you've set.

5-Second Anecdote

One of the most frustrating aspects of leadership is knowing a train wreck is coming but being unable to stop it. I'm thinking about another unit in our organization and a peer of mine, let's call her "Hope For The Best Celeste." Though I have only known her a few years, Celeste has several decades under her belt as a leader. She is a good person, dedicated to our mission, but many have become concerned about her inability to achieve results. Celeste's staff, crucial to our organization's operations, has grown undisciplined in their project execution. If that's not enough, they also lack professionalism. There is one reason for this: for all her good intentions, Celeste continues to rely on a passive approach to performance management. She hasn't taken a key role in setting expectations for her staff and ensuring there are consequences to unmet objectives. It's a problem rather easily resolved, but it requires a paradigm switch in thought and action. I like Celeste, but if she waits much longer to implement change, she is going to laissez-faire herself right out of a job.

Model Behavior

Happy Hour Wisdom

Act in a way that extols the values you aim to promote.

The Ugly Truth

It's not good enough just to talk—leaders act. When you act, make certain you model good behavior. The thought of heightened self-monitoring and editing may sound stifling. It takes effort and discipline, but think of yourself as being in front of the paparazzi, with every move watched and interpreted. If you do something in poor form, people will talk about it. Worse yet, staff may follow your lead and more broadly damage the workings or culture of the organization.

The Bottom Line

Cheer up; this is what you signed up for. You don't need to be perfect, nor does anyone want to see a martyr. In fact, your staff probably would appreciate knowing you have a bit of average Joe or Jane in you. But those whom you lead also need someone to look up to. Most people are looking to be inspired, not just managed. And inspiration comes from being motivated by something positive...you.

Try This

Act like yourself—just a little more self-aware. When you interact with staff, remember that you are a leader. Accord yourself in a way that can be respected. Avoid slipping into unhealthy traps, such as cynicism or personal criticism. We all have problems, but try to hold at bay your neuroticisms, psychotic tendencies, and anti-social behavior. Finally, and though admittedly it's a bit trendy, try to be mindful—leaders need to practice those behaviors that keep us grounded, focused, and thinking and acting in the present.

Beyond that, think of your self-presentation in terms of cooking—adding a dash of this or a dash of that. Show your humanity by throwing in some kindness. Demonstrate you're good-natured with a pinch of humor. Indicate that you are attuned by dishing up a unique recollection about someone or something. Oh, and don't forget to be on time, tell the truth, dress professionally, and avoid gossip. Recall everything else your mom and favorite elementary schoolteacher taught you in order to be an upstanding person.

A Young Fred Rogers

5-Second Anecdote

I have worked with a supervisor, let's call him "Talkative Ted." Ted is a personable leader and very intelligent. I would describe him as an overall caring individual who means well. However, Ted has a big problem, and everyone is aware of it. Ted talks a lot—about people, about their personal problems, their personalities, their work-related shortcomings. Ted is congenial, but I'd wonder what he'd say behind my back! I know his unit and believe that his bad form reflects in the generally rowdy nature of his staff, which contributes, in my opinion, to less than optimal performance. Ted has been around awhile, and he's not likely to change. And as long as he's still there, the dynamics of his organization aren't likely to improve either.

Respect Pays

Happy Hour Wisdom

Respect is the least expensive, and the most important, gift you can give.

The Ugly Truth

It takes time and effort to build and maintain unit morale. You may otherwise be a well-balanced, get-the-job-done, over-achieving type of leader, but don't undervalue the commitment staff needs from you to sustain their trust and dedication. A lack of respect from leaders will reduce motivation, morale, and the opportunity to sustain or build upon your successes.

The Bottom Line

It's back-to-basics time. Honor your staff's right to work in a supportive, nurturing environment and use your energy to create a more positive dynamic. Once you get over the idea that the office isn't just going to right itself without some action on your part, you're on your way to making things better.

Try This

We tend to think about providing respect in simple terms, by treating another with all due esteem—deference, politeness, admiration, etc. While that's true, when respect is fully achieved between leaders and their staff, it includes so much more.

Leader and non-leader relationships are inherently unequal. To demonstrate respect in a real way, you need to go beyond the typical niceties. Start by finding ways—practical to your organization—to value staff for who they are and for what they do. Look for ways to honor them in a way they would expect to be treated.

Within your means, demonstrate generosity and appreciation. For example, are you giving out enough awards? Can you provide (more) training? Can you help facilitate a personal thank-you note from the top leader for a job well done? When's the last time you took a staff member to lunch? How about organizing team building activities? Lastly, on occasion, if the situation warrants, maybe you can afford to be flexible on a rule if an opportunity for a harmless infraction permits.

A Young Ghandi

Also, rediscover what professional happiness means to staff and how intimately it is connected to on-the-job performance and office interactions. You can't force someone to be satisfied, and you certainly don't have the ability to provide everyone with everything that they want. But you can listen. You can be available and accessible to talk about anything your staff needs to talk about, both work and personal.

Take the time to develop more personal relationships. Go desk-to-desk on Monday mornings asking people about their weekends. Remember personal milestones like birthdays and important information like spouses' names and children's names and ages. A well-timed interest in a staff member's personal life ("Is your son feeling better?") or interests ("How was that marathon you ran over the weekend?") can go a long way towards showing you care. Some leaders fear this—mistakenly believing there is or should be a wall between the personal and the professional. The only wall is the one you build.

Also strive to remove barriers between staff and the organization. Respect can include taking the time to help them understand their role in the larger scheme. You as a leader are more plugged into the mission and the vision of the organization than the average team member. You're moving hard and fast, but you generally know why; staff is not as likely to be as connected. They act because they are told to do so—they don't have the same buy-in. So, involve them by sharing with them and providing opportunities for further engagement.

Finally, as you set the tone for a respectful workplace; do so deliberately. Be organized and incremental in your approach. Staff may view you as disingenuous or downright crazy if they see a dramatic change in behavior or unsustainable acts of attention and generosity.

5-Second Anecdote

I once had a supervisor, let's call him "Overhead Oliver." On occasion, Oliver issued interesting taskings that were of questionable urgency and import. Though they didn't hurt, the non-mission essential work taxed staff time in the short term. As a good subordinate, I took Oliver's mission as my own, but I added a kick. Knowing my staff had been down and out due to very high workload, I put a fun spin on Oliver's demands: I attached a prize to the task—an in-office luncheon on me. It was money well-spent, and the relative generosity (it wasn't something I did often), provided some cheer.

Don't Try to Be Popular

Happy Hour Wisdom

Mixing friendship and business is an ill-advised joint venture.

The Ugly Truth

While most of us seek camaraderie in our lives, the complexities of what it takes to build and maintain a friendship don't correspond well with the demand of leading and managing people. There are many more ways for a workplace relationship to go wrong than for such a relationship to go well—and the downside is likely to be detrimental to the organization.

Aside from an outright friendship, conscious or unconscious actions that reflect a need of others to like or approve of you can result in dangerous outcomes for leaders as well. Young leaders eager to build relationships by attempting to please others may be especially vulnerable.

A Young Steve Jobs

The Bottom Line

While the line between work and personal life isn't as rigid as some may believe, it is more important to maintain boundaries when your role is that of a leader. Personal entanglements also complicate your primary loyalty to the organization and your ability to lead others in an equitable manner. The bottom line is that friendship among office peers is okay, but friendship between a leader and a subordinate should be typically avoided.

Try This

In general, and perhaps unfortunately, personal sacrifice is a characteristic largely absent from the echelons of American leadership. If you, as a young, emerging leader can accept the likelihood of subjugating, at times, your own happiness at work, you can set yourself apart. Derive personal satisfaction from doing good work. Take care of people by building relationships among staff, but save gratifying friendships for outside the office confines.

As discussed earlier, it's okay to talk about your weekend and how the kids are doing, but resist the urge to do those things that only friends do. Don't gossip. Celebrate everyone's birthday in a similar way. Don't regularly go to lunch with a single subordinate unless you've offered the opportunity to the entire group. Better yet, instead of one-on-one outings, move towards group team building: happy hours, pot lucks, bowling night—everyone benefits by the social interaction, and you strengthen your organization.

5-Second Anecdote

When I was first promoted into a supervisory leadership position, I found this lesson quite difficult to implement with respect to my friend, let's call her "Best Friend Jen." Logically, I knew what I needed to do—separate myself from her and a couple of other friendships I had built with now-subordinate staff—but I had trouble accepting that things needed to change. I'm a pretty personable fellow, and who doesn't like to be liked? But I did adapt to my new role by becoming someone somewhat different at work—a bit courser, a little less affable. I didn't turn evil, but I laid the groundwork for a certain edge to my work hours self; for example, finding a way to let staff know that when I now made a request, it wasn't a suggestion, it was an expectation. As for my work friendship with Jen, it didn't turn hostile, but it did wane, because I knew I couldn't be popular *and* effective.

Become the Pastor-Boss

Happy Hour Wisdom

Often the most generous form of attention is a friendly ear.

The Ugly Truth

It may be difficult to grasp the entirety of what your staff needs in a supervisor. You have given them training, counseling, respect, resources, and more, and yet—something may be missing. Well, it may surprise (or horrify) you, but you may need to consider providing more intimate care and counsel.

The Bottom Line

There are some intangibles in life; accept it. There is no rulebook for some situations, but you can often intuit your way through certain challenges that manifest themselves in poor morale, poor performance, and poor attitude by broadening your approach to staff counseling.

Try This

I would consider thinking about an intangible approach to counseling when confronted with a situation where something appears amiss with an employee and the genesis of the issue isn't apparent. Try to make the staff member feel at ease—offer a private setting with confidences assured. Create a calm, deliberate approach to the conversation. Ask questions. Listen intently. Don't assume anything. Be prepared to hear intimate workplace or home life confessions. Don't presume you can offer the best advice or assist in resolving everything.

The nature of what I refer to as the "pastor-boss" relationship is that it may lead to a much more personal engagement with employees than some leaders are comfortable with. Talking intimately and honestly is difficult for most people. We are all complicated, often ruled by our emotions. There is no tidy problem-solving methodology to this task, and it may be unclear where to draw the line at an inappropriate conversation. (Certainly do not violate any organizational policies in the course of this effort.) Additionally, it takes some measure of skill to shift in and out of the pastor-boss role (i.e. even when a leader understands the sometimes tragic circumstances of an employee's home life, performance expectations cannot be suspended indefinitely).

The pastor-parishioner and boss-subordinate relationships are comparable in some ways. Both are inherently unequal, with the individual relying on the pastor or boss for guidance, assistance, and evaluation without judgment. As a leader, undertake the challenge with humility. Be genuine and consistent in your approach and patient in your manner.

A Young Dalai Lama

This "touchy-feely" attitude may seem contrary to the image you are building of a resolute and mission-oriented leader, but sometimes good leadership means doing something out of the ordinary. Be that situational leader (see "The Personal Connection" earlier in this part), and one who can demonstrate empathy and care.

Finally, although you may be an occasional backstop for the greater needs of staff, a leader certainly cannot and should not be the center of an employee's effort to cope with an overwhelming challenge not directly related to workplace performance and development. When available and appropriate, suggest use of organizational or community resources (for example, counseling or financial assistance). And regardless of the extent of your dialogue with the individual, always follow up to demonstrate your commitment.

5-Second Anecdote

Many younger, emerging leaders are replacing older bosses who have moved on or retired. I replaced someone; let's call him "Time to Go Joe." Now, Joe needed to move on—he had become timid in the face of needed organizational change, and he was just plain tired. But it was only after he left that I realized he had at least one key attribute that was sorely missed by fellow staff. For all his negatives, over the years Joe had become a patriarch of sorts, a valued resource anyone could turn to for a friendly ear and some reasonable advice. In trying to usher in a new post-Joe era, I was negligent in understanding the full extent of his role. Once I realized this, I attempted to combine the best of my leadership skills with what I knew to be his approachable and empathetic nature. The pastor-boss was born.

Trust but Verify

Happy Hour Wisdom

Trust is a leader's gift to staff…but don't throw away the receipt.

The Ugly Truth

If you have laid the proper groundwork, a young leader must accept the risk inherent in placing confidence in your staff's ability to get the job done right.

A Young Ronald Reagan and Mikhail Gorbachev

The Bottom Line

It's not easy trusting others, and for leaders, who are responsible for everything, it means giving over some measure of control. Trust is important, not only to make possible the spreading of workload, but also because implicit in most every mission is the necessity to develop people. Trusting staff gives them an opportunity to learn new skills and grow professionally, and ultimately succeed or fail in their own right.

Try This

The question of trust in relationships outside of work presents the same challenges and opportunities as trust issues within the workplace. As young leaders, we need to recognize this congruity and take a hard look at developing an organization that emphasizes trust at every level.

Trust is built through many of the practices of good leadership described in this book: two-way communications, transparent actions, giving and seeking advice, offering and receiving support, developing personal bonds, and more. The strongest trust is built over time when both parties see mutual opportunities to grow a stronger relationship. As the leader, assume that most staff wants to do this, as it is in their best interest to work well with the boss. That means the ball is in your court to demonstrate the desire is mutual.

What happens, then, when you come across someone who does not trust or cannot be trusted themselves? For a subordinate, it's a matter of counseling. It's difficult to discipline based solely on "trust," but one should discuss (replete with specific examples) performance issues that reflect a lack of trust. For non-subordinates, work towards developing the relationship, if possible. Be proactive in using the practices above and be especially deliberate in reaching out on a personal level. In all cases where trust is lacking, team building may also help. If all else fails, at least you know the score, and you can calibrate your action/interaction with the individual accordingly.

Finally, the need for a leader to trust is not a license to be naïve. As a leader, it is your job to follow up personally, spot check process or product, question when something seems amiss, and otherwise verify that the work is getting done as well, or better than, planned.

5-Second Anecdote

I once had a subordinate supervisor, let's call him "Lack of Trust Todd." Now Todd had a lot going for him, but he rather candidly admitted that he had "trust issues." I'm all for introspection, but it's very problematic for a leader to have trust issues; it's something that needs to be worked through as soon as possible. Indeed, I came to find that Todd's honesty was well-placed: he obsessively needed to be kept in the loop on most every issue, he attempted to control others, and he tried to game people and issues for his own benefit. The problems were so deep-seated that I pursued a management coach to help guide the counseling that needed to occur. To that end I tried to turn him from "Lack of..." to "Chock Full of...Trust Todd."

Be Prepared to Direct Those Older Than You

Happy Hour Wisdom

Value institutional knowledge; resist institutionalized mindset.

The Ugly Truth

Being a young leader has its challenges, and one of the foremost may be leading people older and more experienced than you. There are a variety of reasons why this occurs and how it manifests. Some may be resentful because you moved up further and faster than they. Others may have preferred someone else in the job. Still more staff may resist being told what to do by someone younger; they may not respect that one so new could possess the knowledge and skill to direct others. These thoughts and feelings may result in attempts to undermine your authority or they may just impede your working relationships. These issues are by no means inherent in everyone and in every organization, but it is a concern you must be prepared to address.

The Bottom Line

The great news is that most older, generally more experienced staff plays a vital role in the success of an organization. Many I've met value their independence but care deeply about the mission and are willing to share vital institutional knowledge. On the downside, other mature workers appear entrenched; they've "seen it all," know the system inside and out, cling to old ways, and may be unwilling—or unable—to change, develop, or mentor others. The bottom line is that we as young leaders need to build competencies that enable us to work with every person as unique individuals.

Try This

Youth or leadership inexperience should never be a cause for a lack of respect, regardless of how old staff is. Act quickly to make age a non-issue by confidently and competently doing your job. You can't demand respect, but use soft, people-oriented skills to win over reluctant staff. Persevere in your efforts.

In everything you do, treat everyone fairly, though not necessarily equitably. It is a supervisor's duty to develop and set expectations for older staff as you would any other. Do so in good faith, and without bias against their ability to grow professionally. As you work with staff, recall the need to be a situational leader—addressing the unique needs of individuals. Older workers often place greater emphasis on certain values such as respect, trust, and loyalty. Beginning with this in mind can provide you an advantage in establishing positive working relationships.

A Young Mark Zuckerberg

Regardless of your constructive efforts to woo older staff, they may simply prefer to be left to do their job, with little input from you. Don't give them special treatment, but don't try to "break" them either. Provide oversight as needed to keep them productive, but also begin succession planning, including an effort to back up their institutional knowledge.

If a thoughtful approach to actively engaging older staff falls short and the detente described above proves impossible, work within your organization's policies and procedures to address issues of performance and/or insubordination. At this point, any intransigence is likely beyond the issue of your youngness or newness. There are many reasons why people, especially older staff, lose motivation. It's also possible leaders who came before you failed to hold individuals accountable. For those who ultimately can't or won't change, I have found the pressure brought about by active performance management (no more or less than you would do for any similarly situated staff) may nudge some entrenched, reluctant retirees towards the next stage in their lives.

Speaking of moving on, for staff-planning purposes it is generally worthwhile to understand when people are eligible to retire and whether they have a date in mind. Note, however, that it is often a discussion that must be delicately approached to avoid the appearance of ageism. For example, as part of a normal counseling session, you might roundly ask if they have a plan to retire in 1-5 years or 5-10 years, etc. Those approaching retirement may also be open to exploring a shift in duties (possibly focused more on knowledge transfer) or even a reduced work schedule. Older staff can provide continuity, and perhaps even flexibility, in workload and workforce management.

Finally, though I've briefly addressed one demographic in this section, know that every age group is generally characterized by a set of values and expectations: a distinct need for engagement, preferred method of communicating, desire for praise, etc. Between Boomers, Generation X'ers and Millennials, as a leader you need to be up on the dynamics of intergenerational workplace issues. If you are not, and you have a diverse workforce, get smart, fast—read up, seek human resource assistance, or find outside consultant services. Also, understand how state and federal law, organizational policy, and any other constraints bear upon the range of staffing decisions available to you.

5-Second Anecdote

I have two staff members, let's call one "Talented Tom" and the other, "Getting By Gary." The former is a very talented individual with many years of experience. He has lost some measure of drive over the years, but he has so much institutional knowledge that there is a lot he has to offer the organization. It's my job to make certain he's in the right seat, performing work that maximizes his abilities and the organization's needs. I looked at Tom's workload and adjusted it to increase mentoring, manage quality assurance, and formalize business processes. I de-emphasized rote paperwork and project leadership.

Gary has put in a lot of years as well, but he is clearly under-performing. He is difficult to work with and his bad habits are entrenched—to the point where he is negatively impacting other staff. I counseled Gary in good faith by setting up clear objectives due at specific dates. I will provide him all due respect but will hold him as accountable as any other staff member. If this doesn't work, we'll have an honest discussion about his options for continuing with or transitioning from the organization. Tom and Gary are from the same generation, but they are approaching their golden years—and impacting the organization—in very different ways.

Fake It, Then Make It

Happy Hour Wisdom

Do. Your. Job.

The Ugly Truth

Sometimes, you just don't know what to do—or how to do it. You may have sought counsel with a mentor or others whom you trust; you've probably educated yourself as much as possible. Yet your instinct is a bust, and you feel overwhelmed. In panic you ask yourself, "What now?"

A Young Che Guevara

The Bottom Line

Being a leader does not require you to know everything, but you always need to be ready to make a decision—and sometimes you need to act before you have all the information that would typically be desirable. Maintain your confidence and your wits, and act logically but decisively.

Try This

Despite being young, leaders of every stripe encounter challenges. There are problem-solving processes. One generalized method follows these steps: (1) properly define the problem; (2) develop alternatives; (3) analyze/assess the alternatives; (4) choose the best course of action with the greatest chance of success; (5) implement the course of action; and (6) review action outcome, correct course if necessary, and/or cement progress.

Move through these steps as deliberately as time will allow. Utilize critical thinking methodologies. Account for your biases. Consider your instincts. Define any risks. Do the necessary research and work with the best people who can assist.

As a young leader working through a problem-solving process in a group setting, be certain you maintain control of the process, and ultimately, the outcome. Others may be looking to you for reassurance; project calm and confidence, even in the face of uncertainty. In the end, no matter the challenge, leaders find a way ahead. If a decision needs to be made under less than desirable circumstances, make the best, most informed decision possible and pursue it with abandon. Be sure to explain your decision to staff so they have greater insight into your process and style. Only modify or change course if there's a good reason to do so. Finally, learn from whatever the outcome.

As a postscript, note that faking it is not a justification for acting rashly or short-circuiting some measure of problem solving or strategic thinking, even when time is short.

5-Second Anecdote

When I was first hired into a leadership position, I was scared. It was the first time I ran such a substantial operation; the first time I supervised people. I lacked formal leadership training, a mentor, and an understanding of the methodologies at my disposal. At my lowest point, I relied solely on the thought that they hired me to do the best job I could do. So, I acted the part—making up my lines as I went along. Sometimes I was confident, most times less so—but my goal was to not let anyone discern the difference. Without me realizing it, over time I faked it less and less, as I learned and internalized the habits of informed decision-making. I made it; so can you.

Engage in What Is Important

Happy Hour Wisdom

Clear head, clear purpose.

The Ugly Truth

It is easy for anyone, including leaders, to get bogged down in rote, time-consuming tasks. Despite all the pressures, good leaders never lose perspective on what it takes to achieve success.

The Bottom Line

Understand the relative importance of all the actions you as a leader are responsible for—from those that are necessary to sustain the organization to those that are required to advance it. Then, be persistent in pursuing critical priorities. The busy work never goes away, but in the end leaders get paid to think and act big.

Try This

More than anything, implementing this lesson involves evaluating and synthesizing several important concepts in this book: mission, time management, task delegation, strategic planning, and more.

Because most leaders direct and oversee the work of subordinates, it is important they not be overtaken by or subsumed into the mechanics of just maintaining the organization itself. In the Army I've heard this referred to as a self-licking ice cream cone. We don't work simply to preserve our ability to continue to work. We work to accomplish something. To accomplish something, we need to understand how our finite time can be spent in undertaking the tasks that will realize our vision for the organization.

The following are examples of questions that leaders who want to engage in what's important, should ask: "What do I as the leader need to prioritize?" "What can be entrusted to my staff?" "Are my people properly trained and otherwise well cared for?" "Do I have a strategic plan?" "What milestones do I need to develop to ensure we are making progress on our long-term goals?" "How can I realize efficiencies to tame the bureaucratic tendencies of my organization?"

Finally, recognize that you as a leader may only oversee one component of your organization's mission. If you are frequently co-opted to help resolve someone else's problems, you're probably a go-to resource and that is flattering. Be a team player, certainly, but consider that in taking on others' responsibilities, you are straining your own ability to engage in what's important to you. Weigh the opportunities and risks of your actions and consider if your priorities are out of balance.

A Young Winston Churchill

5-Second Anecdote

I had a member of my leadership team, let's call him "I'll Get To It Today Ray." Now, Ray is really great—one of the most dedicated members of the organization. He took on an extraordinary amount of responsibility, both on and off the clock. The issue with Ray was not the quantity or the quality of work, it's how he prioritized it. Ray received strategic and urgent taskings from me, lesser but important work from managers, and other ad hoc work from staff. There is also a perpetual workload of cyclical daily, monthly, and annual tasks of varying importance. In truth, the relative priority of things Ray needed to complete varied from day to day. And while Ray had a methodology, it wasn't strategic.

Ray is a people pleaser by nature; he first selected tasks that provided instant gratification by solving problems for others. He is also an arranger—he'd next work on tasks that showcase these talents because he enjoyed them most. For those urgent tasks that Ray couldn't get to because he was working on other things, he'd advise not to worry: "I'll get to it today..." Unfortunately, as with most of us, there's never enough time to do everything. I learned from Ray's example that engaging in what's important is a constant challenge, and it involves overcoming some very strong personal tendencies, but it's a worthy endeavor of a young leader.

Get Used to the Idea That You Will Never Have Enough Time

Happy Hour Wisdom

Take comfort in accepting that which you cannot change.

The Ugly Truth

People are taking numbers outside your office door to speak with you. Your email overfloweth. Your phone is ringing, and it's probably the boss. You took four days of vacation three months ago and still haven't caught up. The walls are closing in around you...welcome to the world of leadership.

The Bottom Line

Don't give in to the chaos, learn to operate within it. Maintain control of your agenda and find ways to optimize your productivity while keeping watch over an ever-growing and changing workload.

Try This

Typically, having a good, productive routine is the best way to keep organized and on top of tasks. However, we all know that when hell rains down on us—and for some that may be daily—all of those good habits are sidelined as we attempt to triage the situation.

I don't have a magic answer to the age-old problem of not enough hours in the day, but here are some tips I use to operate as sensibly as possible.

First, I recognize the situation, and I choose not to panic. How can I remain calm? Well, I've been here before, and I know I'll be here again. There is rarely enough time to do everything perfectly, so I need to try to do really well at most things, most of the time. When perfection is required, I make the time for it.

Next, I attempt to prioritize methodically. I address calls, emails, messages, and the like from those higher up the chain and find a way to respond to their needs or at least acknowledge their communication. I want to keep the boss happy, and besides, any game-changing, critically-important task will usually come from above. Emergency issues with staff also take top priority and will get my quick attention.

For other workload, think about four disposition categories that may provide relief: (1) delegation to staff, (2) delay (i.e., re-prioritize to the bottom of the 'in-box'), (3) improved efficiency (i.e. is there an easy process change that can eliminate or reduce effort on this task), and (4) decline of tasks.

A Young Mother Teresa

With respect to number four, depending on the task and the person requesting that task, it may make sense to politely decline. One should use this sparingly or else be prepared to earn an unflattering reputation. Still, honesty is usually a good route, as we should take pains not to over commit. If your plate is full, but you are indeed the best or only person for the task, you could try to negotiate a due date further in the future. Finally, and I'm sure this goes without saying, take care that if you are a critical link in accomplishing a priority task, fulfill your role so that you aren't holding up the team.

Beyond the above, I recommend reading up on Stephen Covey's time management quadrants as a way to categorize and prioritize different tasks.

5-Second Anecdote

A previous boss, let's call him "Relax Jack" used to say, "Don't sweat the small stuff." It's cliché to be sure, but he didn't just mean "chill." In fact, Jack was a hard-working, focused guy. What he meant was that we should concentrate the majority of our time on the larger, strategic, and more important tasks. He wanted his over-worked, no-relief-in-sight team to seek balance where possible, and to avoid dwelling on that which cannot get done—or perhaps that which cannot get done in the manner we would prefer to do it. He recognized to staff that time was limited and there was no use wishing for more. Jack gave weight to his motto, and he supported staff as they uneasily made their way through the chaos. Thanks, Jack!

The Only Problem is the One Not Anticipated

Happy Hour Wisdom

Think in advance; then, advance.

The Ugly Truth

It's easy to become mired in the issues that we as leaders obsess about day in and day out. However difficult, a good leader needs to think beyond the concerns at hand and focus on what's coming next.

A Young Garry Kasparov

The Bottom Line

Are budget projections off? Are you adequately staffed? Have you thought about your business lines one, two, five years out? A crystal ball would be nice, but without it, a good leader still needs to anticipate the next big thing. The sooner young leaders acclimate themselves to this expectation, the better. Potential issues need to be identified and given adequate attention early—before they become large problems or missed opportunities.

Try This

The anticipation required here takes an aggressive, almost maniacal ability to look all around and up and down the organization. Those who best approach this quest are puzzle-solvers, chess players, sleuths, and others who think broadly, are unafraid of a challenge, and intrigued by creative problem solving.

Indeed, think of it as a game. Get out there before anyone else. Find the problem early: analyze it, strategize potential courses of action, take action if it's within your immediate control and report up your chain of command if it's not.

And of course, if the challenge is big, remember the basics. Don't panic, just prepare. Organize around a game plan. Secure needed resources. Stick to a schedule. If additional help is needed, approach higher level leadership with potential solutions—not just problems.

Win the game by advancing your mission to the next level of success.

5-Second Anecdote

I know a leader, let's call him "Give His All Paul." Paul is a well-respected individual in the organization—he has been around awhile, knows everyone well, and is absolutely committed to the mission. What makes Paul special is his willingness to tackle a problem before it becomes a fashionable topic of conversation. For example, I remember him talking to me passionately about the need to build our bench by recruiting new talent and truly integrating them into the organization. He not only identified an issue that would become a priority of our organization, but he took the reins of the program to ensure its success. Paul saw the problem coming and went out of his way to notify higher leadership and work a solution. Leaders like Paul inspire me to continue to work hard, develop, and be an integral part of achieving our organization's vision.

Stay the Right Course

Happy Hour Wisdom

A sense of direction keeps you on the path to success.

The Ugly Truth

Maybe you have read the previous pages, and you are energized to lead your own revolution. That's great, but don't confuse the need to act in a decisive and impactful way—in order to get results—with the patience necessary to stay fixed on a good course of action. Changing your mind often and acting hastily produces disarray and jeopardizes mission accomplishment.

The Bottom Line

Good leaders have patience and take a long view because they know getting it right matters. These leaders aren't swayed by fear of failure and only contemplate making a tactical move when they conclusively determine the present course will not achieve success.

Try This

This lesson is about active decision-making and emotional fortitude. When you arrive at a juncture that requires either action or inaction, seriously consider the benefits of staying the course.

When leaders do not act, it is either out of negligence (they don't know what to do or they do not care to do what it takes) or because they make an active decision that inaction is the best course of action.

Maintaining the status quo may seem like a contradiction in a book that touts leadership as a means to affect change. But there's no double-speak here—young leaders must recognize the raw power in making a deliberate decision to act. That decision, to positively influence events, is a determination that the status quo will not achieve the desired results. A decision to act usually feels fulfilling because it is dynamic, and leaders by definition play the central role in orchestrating mission accomplishment.

Of course some actions involve successive and inter-related decisions. A decision to act may produce results that call for either inaction or further action. Each step requires problem solving and decision-making to some extent. But at each step, we as young leaders should look at the issue anew, take a step back and dispassionately reassess the operating environment, and carefully determine the next course of action. Maybe the situation needs more time. Perhaps there are variables in play that make further action unwise. Maybe the matter is no longer an issue.

The key is to fight the urge to make a fast or imprudent decision and rigorously analyze the "no action" option. Gather and assess information. Seek the wise counsel of staff. Consider risk. Think creatively and strategically. Pace yourself if there is time to do so by resisting efforts to arrive at a seemingly easy, premature, or consensus decision.

A Young Teddy Roosevelt

5-Second Anecdote

I remember a time, early on in my leadership career, when I needed to resolve a serious personnel issue. I was being advised by multiple people, including our very experienced and sharp-tongued labor counselor, let's call her "Sharp Wit Kit." The problem at hand involved an employee's violation of policy in a very public setting and in a way that reflected poorly on the organization. In making a decision on the consequences of the individual's actions, Kit advised me on a seemingly clear and definitive decision to punish him. I thought about the issues, but I had reservations. I feared the situation was in danger of becoming a high profile, media-driven public spectacle, and that pressing our rather technical conduct violation would only worsen the matter. Kit demurred, and I ultimately decided to act to punish the individual instead of exercising patience and perhaps eventually pursuing a lower-key resolution. Of course the matter did indeed blow up, and I wished I had trusted my gut and stayed the course.

Maintain Balance

Happy Hour Wisdom

A balanced life is a happy and prosperous one.

The Ugly Truth

Finding balance includes building and enjoying a satisfying personal life. This isn't easy, as I'm certain you know. As someone who's earned success, you've probably had to give up some things along the way. Know that it is never too late to start anew...or to make up for lost time. It does, however, take effort.

A Young Sheryl Sandberg

The Bottom Line

Having a life outside work—family, friends, and hobbies—will help you achieve greater contentment. Well-grounded and well-rounded leaders are poised for success because their fulfillment yields greater confidence, more focus, and a better ability to connect with people.

Try This

Get into a routine—make a schedule that gives you time for a personal life—and stick to it. Creating routine helps us sort out and limit time and energy dedicated to certain rote tasks and acts as a forcing mechanism by reserving space for other meaningful endeavors we might not otherwise prioritize. Consider coming in early, leaving early, and having some time to do things before the sun goes down. Or, maybe you'd rather exercise first and come in a little later. Why not sometimes use designated breaks and lunches for a non-work respite, like reading or meeting a friend. All job responsibilities are different, of course, but during non-work hours try to limit work-related tasks.

Don't think of yourself as having two separate components of your life, one on and one off the clock. If you've made private and professional choices that reflect your values and goals, an integrated life of work and home is possible through a little effort. If you are really out of balance, righting yourself may involve a serious discussion with higher level leaders. If you are working at an unsustainable pace, they hopefully have as much interest as you in avoiding your burnout.

And finally, remember that enjoying life goes beyond succeeding as a leader…it means being happy.

5-Second Anecdote

I had a boss, let's call him "Overworked Burke," a really good leader who was always on task. He was living the dream—wonderful children, great spouse, friends, and lots of non-work interests. At the office, he worked very hard. He delegated some tasks, and that's good, but he was also very detail-oriented, almost obsessed with the minutiae. In the process of not wanting to leave any stone unturned, Burke logged an incredibly high number of hours and at some point he completely lost balance, working all hours of the night and weekend. As the supervisor, many others began to follow his unhealthy lead. Burke faced exhaustion and illness, and he eventually backed off his unrealistic schedule. Interestingly, his case illustrates that those who lose balance do so for a variety of reasons as well. He apparently wasn't using work as an escape or as an attempt to get ahead. Burke just became overwhelmed and tried to keep up by doing more—and that doesn't always work. Happily, he changed course before any permanent harm was done. He's now "Burke in Balance."

Keep Critical Distance

Happy Hour Wisdom

Maintain a level head and a distant heart.

The Ugly Truth

For young leaders, "critical distance" represents the emotional divide that separates you and your work. Sometimes emotion is okay, but when it's not, it may overpower the critical thinking and relationship-building skills you need to be an effective leader.

The Bottom Line

Certainly leaders are not above attaching feeling to a given issue or situation. Despite this, leaders must be very aware that when an emotional response is excessive, inappropriate, ill-timed, or delivered to the wrong audience, it may produce unintended negative consequences. For example, passion is good, but too much enthusiasm may seem inauthentic. Communicating frustration may be necessary, but degrading staff is not okay. Staff want to see a leader firmly in control of themselves, acting logically, and confident about the course ahead.

Try This

Attaining critical distance requires an advance commitment by a leader to minimize emotional connection to one's work or specifically with respect to a given matter. This very decision requires a self-awareness that alone represents a positive step taken in the development of a heightened, leadership-oriented self-control. Ideally, critical distance would help prevent clouded thought, rash decisions, and unwise outbursts. For many, it takes deliberate effort to be present or mindful, in the moment, when an emotional response could be triggered.

Triggers can occur in a variety of forms. Sometimes negative feelings result from someone violating an important value we hold. Other times someone presses you on a "hot-button" issue, a topic that, for whatever reason, causes a visceral response. People themselves may be hot-buttons if we negatively associate them with someone or something. Awareness of your values and hot-buttons can provide time for a leader to pause and intellectually consider a response before emotions intervene. It also diminishes the ability of others to manipulate your triggers.

Understand, however, that critical distance does not mean acting like you are dead inside. Emotion is good and necessary. Leaders must possess the capacity to lead or join others in the heartfelt expression of feelings: joy over the birth of a child, elation in the landing of a big account, or grief over the loss of loved one. Staff wants to know they are led by real people—they want to be able to relate to you. However, they also prefer to hold their leaders in esteem. To balance this, seek to cultivate a style that is genuine, but tempered.

A Young Martin Luther King, Jr.

Finally, note that a job of the leader—especially a middle level one—is to occasionally shelter staff from overwrought emotion and other turbulence coming from higher leadership or elsewhere within the organization. To some extent, this involves maintaining critical distance *for others*—protecting staff from trivial or distracting things. Other times, you just need to consider a more positive way to translate direction from others in the leadership chain. To wit, if you as a leader can only motivate staff by saying "The big boss is angry," you need to consider additional tools to influence your people.

For many, achieving critical distance takes practice. If you need help calibrating a response, don't fret; seek counsel from close advisers, friends, or peers, if necessary.

Five Second Anecdote

I had been in my leadership job for several years when a new head of the organization, let's call him "Promote Him Tim," came along. He was more surface than substance. With people like that, my expectations for actual leadership plummet, and I pretty much just hope long-lasting damage to the organization is limited. Not to be. Though ours had been a generally transparent organization with merit-based hiring and promotion procedures, Tim began to elevate a small cadre of cronies around him. One person in a position to know said Tim would simply identify an individual and instruct HR to "promote him." These folks had nothing going for them except access. Now, we knew Tim wasn't going to be around the organization for long, but these people, several of whom were put in positions of leadership, would have an impact for years.

I felt helpless, almost distraught. I worked within channels to support others who knew about Tim's improprieties and were attempting to hold him accountable. At a certain point, however, the bad news was coming faster than potential relief, and I decided I needed to emotionally distance myself from the matter. I wish I had done so sooner. I respect my original outrage, but there's nothing it accomplished that I couldn't have done without a bit more dispassion. In hindsight, I think the matter touched on an important value of mine—fairness—and probably even a hot-button issue—competent leadership. When those were violated, I became emotionally involved, and I lost the healthy separation between my feelings and my work.

Don't Hesitate to Follow-Up to Get What You Need

Happy Hour Wisdom

Follow-up to successfully close out.

The Ugly Truth

There are lots of ugly ways to get people to move faster: threats, coercion, unpleasant working conditions, etc. None of these are appropriate leadership tools, of course. So, after coordinating with someone to complete a task, and if they haven't met set expectations, you must take initiative to get them back on track. As a leader, the buck stops with you.

The Bottom Line

To keep up with an often overwhelming workload, a leader uses anyone at his or her disposal to assist: delegating tasks to subordinates, collaborating with peers, and even getting your boss to move on something. If time is running short, and someone owes you on a project you own, follow-up... fast.

Try This

It's not enough to say "It's in John's court." You can't just insist, "Mary owes me a call." Leaders don't make excuses or place blame— they do what's necessary to get the job done.

Leaders not only assign and coordinate work; they also ensure everything gets completed on time and to specifications. Carefully track the requirements that have been set and call, email, text, or show up in person to make a contact with whoever has the task. No hesitation or procrastination—just do it. It's a part of a leader's responsibility to make certain the mission succeeds by ensuring that everyone does their part. When someone is remiss in their work, there are probably reasons, and some of them might even be acceptable. Deal with the delay, but also be dogged: work with the person or team to reset expectations, and return again to ensure the work is complete.

5-Second Anecdote

I once knew a team leader, let's call him "I'm Done David." The problem, as you might guess, is that he finished with his component of a multi-part project and considered his work complete. David vociferously argued that he couldn't force others on the team to do their work. He avoided confronting and holding others accountable. I challenged David to actively follow-through on the project. I encouraged him to both communicate with staff so that everyone shared the same expectations, and then use all proper means to ensure the job got done right. And then I followed-up with him to make certain he did it.

Give Senior Leaders What They Need; Get Back in Return

Happy Hour Wisdom

Help your leader, help yourself.

The Ugly Truth

No matter who you are, you have a boss—even the most important leader reports to someone. And your leader expects you to deliver in a timely manner. Get to it.

A Young Sun Tzu, Renowned Chinese General

The Bottom Line

With all the competing demands on our time, young leaders need to prioritize—we know that. In this process, some tasks or projects will get downgraded. Those that reflect the priorities of senior leaders—whether expressly stated or implied—must not be among those relegated to the dreaded queue. Do them first. Do them well. Do them with a smile. The return is worth it.

Try This

Giving the boss what he or she asks for is of equal importance to giving the boss what they need. Giving your leader what they need takes skill. Attempt to be a partner, a confidante, and a source of counsel. Try to help him or her succeed. Be proactive. Be thorough. Troubleshoot ideas. There are so many ways you as a leader can grow in your own right by effectively serving someone your senior.

If you've already concluded your boss is not redeemable as a competent leader, just try your best to work in good faith. Learn what you can, work hard, get noticed by others, and make a move when the time is right. If your boss has decided you are not redeemable, try to determine why and what you can do differently. Working in good faith against all odds may not make a believer out of your current boss, but hopefully other leaders will take note of your efforts. Again, learn what you can and make a move when the time is right.

5-Second Anecdote

I mentored one aspiring leader, let's call him "Over His Head Oliver." Oliver had a tough time balancing the overwhelming demands of his position. I felt for him—there was just not enough time in the day to get everything done that he was being asked to do. For Oliver, the very thought of to-do items piling up on his list or in his in-box was driving him mad. I advised him to meet with his boss and discuss his performance objectives. I encouraged him to have a thorough give-and-take so they both had a shared understanding as to his workload. But I also emphasized that Oliver should not simply look at his objectives as boxes to be checked, but as opportunities to learn and be a part of his boss's leadership journey. This wasn't a quick road to happiness for him, but he did persevere, and he did develop. The situation ended up being optimal for Oliver.

It's Okay to Ask Senior Leaders For Help

Happy Hour Wisdom

When you reach out, don't forget to reach up.

The Ugly Truth

Leadership challenges are many, and you have to make use of every resource available to you…and certainly nothing can rival the input of those with the most experience. Don't be proud—ask for help.

The Bottom Line

Some young leaders believe that asking for assistance gives the appearance of weakness or vulnerability. And don't get me wrong, acting entitled, whiny, or needy is a recipe for unemployment. The key here is that good leaders engage in continual learning, and this includes seeking advice or assistance—in moderation. We've discussed mentors and sponsors, but don't forget your boss, and any other senior leader that may appear open to being of service.

Try This

The best organizations understand the need to develop leaders from within. This includes senior leaders helping junior leaders hone their skills. A good first option would be your direct supervisor. Who better to teach you what 'right' looks like than the person who evaluates your performance? If that won't work, broaden your search to others inside or outside your organization.

Whomever you approach, how do you actually ask for help? Don't be too hard on yourself ("I'm just stupid or something—I can't figure this one out…"). Don't be too needy, either ("Man, you have to help me—I'm desperate!"). Just be humble and sincere ("Gail, I was wondering—if you have time later—could I bounce some thoughts off you?").

After the leader has accepted your request for input, make certain you tell him or her your thought process—show that you've done some legwork on resolving the issue, and that you've developed possible courses of action. Engage meaningfully, and seriously consider any advice provided to you. Of course, thank the leader for his or her time.

It might be wise to follow up after the fact as well—to further develop the relationship.

A Young Nelson Mandela

Most people in general, and leaders in particular, enjoy the thought of sharing their knowledge with others. Take advantage of this opportunity—not just to solve a problem, but to learn and grow professionally.

5-Second Anecdote

I once knew a leader, let's call her "Stuck in the Sand Pam." We all disliked working with Pam as she was generally behind the power curve. If she didn't complete a task, she wouldn't just admit to it; if she was unaware of a policy, she wouldn't just seek it out; and finally, if she needed help, she wouldn't just ask for it. Pam would struggle through issues instead of confronting them aggressively, asking for help when needed, and then just finishing the job. The bottom line is that Pam wasn't honest with herself (and others) about her limitations; otherwise, she and the organization would be a lot be a lot less stuck.

Part IV. I'm Looking To Impress

Understand the Difference Between a Leader and a Manager

Happy Hour Wisdom

A manager runs what a leader builds.

The Ugly Truth

There is more to being in charge than just making the trains run on time. Minutes and hours are precious, and those who do not deliberately take the time to do the work of leaders are not doing right by their people and the organization.

A Young Henry Ford

The Bottom Line

Managers are at the operational level. They implement plans. Leaders operate at a higher, more strategic level. They develop plans and ensure successful implementation. All leaders are managers, to some extent. Not all managers, however, are leaders. When you are ready to move to that next level, reach beyond the skills that are typically associated with competent managers (schedules are set, people are paid, supplies are stocked, tasks are accomplished). Those organization and coordination skills are important, but it is the aspirational and potentially transformational goals that comprise the heart and mission of a leader.

Try This

If your daily schedule seems limited to batting down emails, pushing papers, and responding to the whims of any staff member who happens to pass your office, you're not doing enough leader work. Think about upping your game. Refer back to "Achieve Strategic Depth" (Part II) and "Engage in What's Important" (Part III). Look forward to "Understand Strategic Planning and Think Long Term," later in this part. Some of these concepts overlap, but it's impossible to overstate the extent to which leaders must understand what they are doing (or not doing) and employ the right skills to advance the cause of the organization

In my personal journey, I have found it useful to consider the challenge of leadership in multiple ways, including that of manager vs. leader. Becoming a leader takes time. Leadership principles are many and varied, and they require constant honing. Those who aim to move beyond basic management—either in their present job or in the next— must challenge themselves to consistently and persistently act the part.

5-Second Anecdote

I once knew a Project Manager, let's call her "Eager Emily." Emily aspired to be a leader. She went through the usual motions: leadership development course, mentorship, and multiple experiential opportunities. She was a careful study and she had drive, but just going through the motions wasn't enough. It proved difficult for Emily to let go of her narrowly-focused management skills. She was obsessively drawn to detail, preoccupied with immediate goals, and she hued very closely to established orthodoxy. Over time, and with plenty of trial and error and some intense self-reflection, Emily developed a solid set of leadership skills. Her journey could have begun with an understanding that success in leadership requires a different plane of thought and action; one that is distinguished from pure management.

Overachieve

Happy Hour Wisdom

Success always.

The Ugly Truth

Leaders succeed by constantly pushing to be the best. Not your best—
the best.

A Young Frank Lloyd Wright

The Bottom Line

Try, fail, try…succeed. Then succeed again and again. It may take
time, but as a leader, you need to be the one who makes the difference.
Success is what leaders do, period. There should be some comfort here;
it's a clear objective. Set big goals and make plans to achieve them. Be
zealous in your pursuits.

Try This

This lesson isn't about meeting a metric; it's about coming in first place in the only race that matters. Leaders don't just care-take an organization—they commit the time and will to do the work necessary to accomplish the mission. Don't rely on your competitors to under-perform. Ensure you are doing enough of the right work to overshoot the goal.

Overachievement can also be adrenaline-producing. Use it to push harder and further. Recall your wins. Write them down. Tell others. It's not an ego thing—give credit where it's due and always share more glory than necessary. Just remember how satisfying the win feels. Young leaders need to fill their quiver with successes—both to prove their worth and to have something to build upon.

5-Second Anecdote

I had a leader, let's call him "Always Pushing Peter." He was the epitome of a can-do spirit, and no matter the challenge, he always wanted to come out on top. In motivating staff, he'd talk about the importance of winning. Even in the face of long odds, he'd simply say, "How are we going to get this done?" And if the strategy at hand didn't appear aggressive enough, Peter would jump in with his own plan, becoming personally engaged when necessary. He was tough, and it was exhausting to work for him, but with his drive, Pushing Peter Plucked a Peck of Success.

Do the Hard Stuff

Happy Hour Wisdom

Do yourself what others won't.

The Ugly Truth

Face and embrace the mess of difficult day-to-day leadership challenges; it's part of the job.

The Bottom Line

Whereas "overachieve" is about a focus on success; this lesson emphasizes the reality of the tough, unfun, and less-than-glamorous tasks it takes to get there.

A Young Mike Rowe

Try This

Fear-producing public speaking, insane spreadsheets and endless data, firing staff, impossible deadlines, risky decisions, irate senior leaders, demanding customers...these are but a few of the hard things young leaders will address. Don't shrink from any of it!

Psych yourself up with the metaphor of your choosing: climb a mountain, slay a dragon, soar like an eagle, reach for the stars, and even battle your demons. Or stick with the clichés of the trade: get out of your comfort zone, think out of the box, make it happen, or fire on all cylinders. Whatever your self-talk, work yourself up to the challenge. It takes strength of mind to confront, and dedication to see through, the difficult things. Limit distractions and focus your efforts. Problem solve. Break tasks into smaller, more manageable parts with reasonable deadlines. Create incentives when you achieve milestone accomplishments. Lean on others for help.

Granted, sometimes the perks just don't seem to balance against the stress of the job. But remember: you chose the challenge of leading, and the gratification of achieving the mission and the opportunities to learn that come with the struggle provide lasting fulfillment. Finally, think of the hard stuff as special and worthwhile because they represent the unique work of leaders.

5-Second Anecdote

Everyone probably knows someone like a colleague with whom I've worked, let's call her "Just Enough Justine." Justine seems to embrace her own leadership title more than the work itself. She doles out business cards like candy. Yet Justine's repertoire of tasks is limited: she attends meetings (often late), inputs into conversations superficially, and otherwise spends her days giving vague direction in a slightly cynical manner. Aside from what may be a less-than-great attitude, it's not evident to me that she pulls her weight: a lack of follow through on strategic initiatives, no accountability of staff, and little supervision of critical teams under her management. One can only coast for so long. If she doesn't start doing the hard stuff soon, she'll be "Just Gone Justine."

Be Innovative

Happy Hour Wisdom

Think anew.

The Ugly Truth

Generally speaking, a young leader has less experience to draw upon, and thus less ability to contextualize and strategize problems as they arise. This puts us at a disadvantage.

A Young Shigeru Miyamoto, Japanese Video Game Designer and Producer

The Bottom Line

While younger, emerging leaders may lack organizational history and experience, they are capable of fresh thinking—and that might be just as powerful, if not more so. Newer leaders bring creativity, a critical eye, and the energy needed to burst paradigms, push boundaries, and resolve complex issues. Innovation is among the greatest values you bring to your organization.

Try This

Leaders who succeed at innovation question almost everything. Imagine the future by opening your mind to different possibilities. Don't accept mediocre processes or products. Challenge assumptions. Rethink the status quo. Bring creativity to everyday tasks.

When you generate ideas, some will prove workable, others will not. Don't shrink from this process. Accept the vulnerability and risk of proposing ideas that may be rejected or fail. When it's necessary to do so, work change subtly to achieve influence.

You say you're not the innovative type? Leaders only need to know where innovation is needed to gain efficiency or effectiveness. From there, encourage a culture where other leaders and staff engage openly and honestly about ideas and options. Leaders should bring energy and resources to this process.

5-Second Anecdote

I had an incredibly innovative superior, let's call him "Rethink Rick." What made this guy so valuable to the organization was his ability to approach each issue with a fresh perspective. I remember one particular time we were on deadline to resolve a particularly sticky issue with a client. A group of us looked at the problem from all angles, but we were stuck. Rick, full of happy determination, joined in and began to troubleshoot options aloud. It turned into a great brainstorming effort. No one was pre-occupied with being right; there was no pride of ownership. We just wanted to get to (and eventually we did find) a solution that worked. When I sometimes feel as though I've reached a creative dead end, I ask myself "What would Rick do?"

Take Risks

Happy Hour Wisdom

Well-considered venture can be met with reward.

The Ugly Truth

Consider that leaders are often made great by taking advantage of the opportunities that arise. However, the ugly truth is that we can't always anticipate when, where, and how those moments of potential reward will manifest themselves.

The Bottom Line

As a young leader, you must be agile in anticipating the need and opportunity for risk-taking. Risk involves the often difficult prospect of accepting uncertainty—that's why not everyone can embrace it. Leaders, however, must accept that weighing and acting on risk, where prudent to do so, allows one to take advantage of opportunity (or the minimization of threat) to the advantage of the organization.

Try This

The balancing of risk and reward can be more analytic (a quantitative risk assessment) or not (compare the benefits of the risk's success in a "plus" column, against the costs in a "negative" column). The analytic side more expressly considers the size of the potential downside and the likelihood that it will occur. Whatever the method—and there are multiple out there—be honest and realistic in assessing potential variables. Calculate what an acceptable risk is so that you know your chances of success going in. Gamble when the need is there, and the chances of success are worth the risk; be cautious when it's not.

As part of your decision-making process, think several steps ahead—about both success and failure. If success, then what? How do you build on that? If failure, then what? How do you mitigate the damage? Don't discount your gut feelings. Good leaders have honed instincts that may provide an indefinable weight on the scale in one direction or another. Bring in outside counsel—leaders, consultants, etc. when necessary.

Finally, risk-taking can stimulate adrenaline and produce an energetic high. It's okay to promote an adventurous ethos for your organization and to use this to motivate and challenge staff. As a young leader, however, maintain proper perspective and know when the risk/reward doesn't balance out.

A Young Harvey Milk

5-Second Anecdote

I knew a manager, let's call her "Play It Safe Suzy." Now Suzy is a rock solid individual—good people skills, very productive, a leader I'd want on my team. I noticed, however, that when she makes decisions, she tends to the more conservative side. For example, let's say Suzy is short-staffed, but she is confronted with a high profile client who has a priority project. There are several options: (1) one manager might redirect resources at the expense of other workload to meet the client's challenge; (2) another manager might deliver bad news to the client that workload cannot be adjusted, and his project cannot be expedited; and (3) a final manager might work with the client, understand his bottom line, and strive to accommodate his timeframe while seeking additional resources (more staff, overtime pay). Suzy would tend towards #2, the more passive option, and the one that perhaps risks less by allowing the status quo to play out. The flipside is that there is no chance of reward—of pushing oneself and staff to find a way to ensure customer satisfaction. By playing it safe, Suzy won't save the day.

Have a Vision

Happy Hour Wisdom

Look forward to the future.

The Ugly Truth

You cannot lead without formulating a direction in which to take people.

The Bottom Line

Formulating, communicating, and following through on a vision is one of the toughest jobs of a leader, and there is no script to see you through this important task. Vision is developed through focus on the unique competencies of the organization, and it serves an important purpose in keeping it healthy and dynamic.

A Young John F. Kennedy

Try This

To envision is to look forward—to imagine the future of the organization as you the leader see it. I've heard this described as a picture developed in the leader's mind that he or she then shares with others. Even as young leaders, perhaps representing component parts of an organization, we should attempt to visualize and describe how we see the future.

For staff, a vision can be an incredible rallying point—a way to connect to the leader's passion, feel pride in the organization, and motivate them in their work. Because of its importance, careful attention should be paid in talking about vision to staff and nesting the organization's goals in it.

A leader's vision may reflect or derive from the organization's vision statement. The vision statement is a short, simple, and clear declaration of what the organization aspires the future to be. While a leader conceives of his or her own vision, a vision statement can and probably should be developed with broader input. Note that a vision statement is contrasted with a mission statement, which explains to others what it is special that an organization does.

5-Second Anecdote

I had a senior leader who was an incredible visionary, let's call him "Forward-Leaning Fred." All this guy did was contemplate the future. He was so far ahead in his thinking, he was scarcely credible in the present. Fred sometimes had trouble connecting up his vision to the mission. He knew where he wanted us to be, but not always how we were going to get there. He confused and exhausted staff. At times he proved too willing to abandon core organizational values in the process of achieving his goals. The point here is that care must be taken in striving to realize one's vision. Fred taught me about articulating the future, and I'm grateful for that, but the upheaval he brought about affected the organization for years after his departure.

Understand Strategic Planning and Think Long-Term

Happy Hour Wisdom

Thinking ahead is key to not being left behind.

The Ugly Truth

Resting on or basking in where you are at this moment is a recipe for decay. A leader's most pressing challenge is to ensure his or her organization is on (or remains on) a path towards success.

The Bottom Line

Strategic planning is where the magic happens...this is when you get to be a leader and not just a manager. Think beyond the day-to-day running of the organization and focus on shaping it years into the future. It's a glorious opportunity to transform or propel your organization forward.

Try This

Strategic planning is the sum of the essential components that define your organization: mission, vision, strategy, goals, core values, and a host of other things not covered in these pages.

To accomplish the planning, develop a plan. This can be done in multiple ways depending on the size and complexity of your organization. First, choose how it will be done and who will do it. Confer with in-house experts and/or outside consultants if necessary. Next, understand who you are as an organization. This can be done fairly easily via a "SWOT" analysis that captures strengths, weaknesses, opportunities, and threats. Contemplate both internal and external influences. Next, focus on what your organization does best and analyze how you can innovate and grow from there. The plan will include additional detail, including both short and long-term objectives.

Once you make progress in planning, keep the momentum going. Communicate your work up and down the chain of command and to staff. Get feedback and buy-in. Ensure implementation by nesting individual performance goals within the objectives laid out in the plan. Provide the time and resources to ensure success. Measure accomplishments incrementally and through the use of individuals (we call them "champions") assigned to oversee progress. Provide regular, ongoing follow-up.

5-Second Anecdote

I used to have a boss, let's call him "Contemplate Tate." Tate was obsessed with short and long-term strategic planning. At the time, I didn't fully appreciate the more or less continual need to review the organization and plan for the future. Cynically, I just saw one more plan with a slogan that required memorization and feigned enthusiasm. Once I made it to the inner circle, I saw how strategy develops. It was like preparing a dinner feast—messy, spirited, and certainly a process. Tate demanded that all his top cooks be in the kitchen to assist. In the end, we were left with something big to chew on: a solid understanding of where we were going to take the organization. That was the "aha" moment when I realized the value of strategic planning. I also learned that the top-down ability to engage and convert others to this cause was a measure of a leader's skill. He might as well be called "Great Tate."

Learn Something from Everyone and Everything

Happy Hour Wisdom

Keep your mind open.

The Ugly Truth

Leadership is one of those fields where there is a lot to understand, and you usually need to learn it fast so that you can use it immediately. One of my past leaders used to call this 'building an airplane in flight.' There's just so much out there to learn from—developing some measure of wisdom may be easier said than done.

The Bottom Line

It's doable. We as young leaders need to be open to finding and absorbing the elements of wisdom that surround us. Key lessons can be found everywhere—in articles, books, television shows, even casual conversations. Some lessons are big and thought-provoking. Others are small and easily relatable. All are part of the puzzle.

Try This

Keep it fun. Don't be overwhelmed by too much information and too much advice. Focus on the essential, often the simple. Don't force the pieces together; grow at your own pace. The result will be a deeper, more comprehensive perspective on leadership.

Keep in mind that many great lessons are found outside traditional business and leadership sources. Leadership is very much an exploration of the self, of others, and of life. I've articulated my belief that though leaders and leadership are profoundly impacting, we lack a shared vocabulary and a shared understanding that might enable an effective dialogue on the subject. In its absence, metaphors for leadership seem to turn up frequently.

Finally, be interested in others—even those who may not fit a traditional, successful, leader mold. We as individuals are on distinct paths, and what we do produces incredibly different lessons. I'm grateful when others are willing to share their experiences. And once you come across a new nugget of learning that you can apply to your leadership journey, do what it takes to remember it—make a note, keep a journal, etc.

5-Second Anecdote

When I became a supervisor and embarked on a serious study of leadership, I quickly learned that I needed a more efficient system of taking in and processing information. My memory is only mediocre, but there was more to it. I discovered I was taking in great lessons and great advice, but I didn't always need it when I received it. So, I began to find ways to put the pieces of my puzzle together. I created an online journal of lessons learned; I wrote down quotes I liked and books that were recommended to me. Beyond this book, my studious note-taking continues!

Know Your Personal Inventory

Happy Hour Wisdom

> *The key to growth is better understanding who you are,*
> *what you do, and why you do it.*

The Ugly Truth

If someone else figures you out (for example, your biases, your weaknesses, your motivations) before you have done so yourself, you're in trouble.

The Bottom Line

The goal is to see yourself as you actually are (or close as is possible) and to use what you know to enhance your own effectiveness as a young leader.

When I write about personal inventories, I refer to broad categories of testing that include personality-type assessments measuring everything from how one communicates, to how one approaches problem solving, and more. Examples include "StrengthsFinders," "Meyers Briggs," "Social Styles," and a multitude of 360-degree assessments.

The key here is to understand that we are complex beings who are generally bound to patterns of thought and behavior. These tendencies reflect the core of our life's circumstances, relationships, and experiences. Personal inventory assessments help us better understand ourselves for the purpose of facilitating self-learning, improving our interactions with others, and recognizing when our cognitive or emotional habits impede what's possible in our personal and professional growth.

Try This

Becoming a well-rounded leader involves a healthy dose of humility. Leaders, who provide constructive performance-related feedback to subordinates, must be able to self-diagnose as well. That includes understanding a real and complete picture of yourself, positive and otherwise. A leader seen to be improving or adapting his or her self also generates credibility.

Aside from undertaking the assessments, encourage others to do so as well. Consider using organizational resources—time and funding—

to reach more staff. Facilitators can help implement testing and interpret results. Use what is learned to set personal and professional goals for individuals and teams. Depending on the assessment, staff/leaders should be encouraged to share results as a means of creating greater openness and transparency across the organization.

5-Second Anecdote

As a young leader on an important project (that was somehow already behind schedule, mired in complex issues, and lacking in sufficient funding), I became responsible for a team of diverse individuals. There's the quiet but smart one, the social one, the one who is less apt to go the extra mile, and the one who is eager, but doesn't know why he's on the team. In anticipation of our first meeting, I sized up the team and considered the potential roles and responsibilities of its members. I then asked myself, "Where on Earth do I begin?" Just call me "Where to Start Mark."

I began by assessing the team with respect to technical ability and emotional intelligence. In this case, these folks hadn't taken personal inventories, and time-wise we couldn't afford to pause and do that.

However, I tried to assess their strengths and weaknesses and set up responsibilities accordingly. The smart but quiet one? She was my second-in-command, with special roles as note-taker, time-keeper, and schedule-master. The social one? He was my point of contact to the external customer, and internally, I asked him to craft the occasional team-building exercise or work break. The 9-5, stay-in-my-lane one? I made her the workhorse in charge of generating the necessary but less-than-glamorous data, upward reporting, and regulatory requirements. The eager confused one? With group input he took on the task of gathering research and drafting project documents. I'm not saying it resolved everything, but assessing the team first gave me a start.

Stay Focused on the External

Happy Hour Wisdom

Look out—opportunity or challenge may come from any direction.

The Ugly Truth

As a leader, most of your day may be spent working internal matters: policies and procedures, staffing, budget and project meetings, reporting up the chain of command, etc. Sometimes we are so focused on routine operations, we neglect the larger picture, including those external events and relationships that may, in the long run, drive customers or funding, public sentiment, operational improvements, and more.

A Young Aaron Swartz

The Bottom Line

As young leaders we need to remember that, with respect to the outside world, we don't work in isolation. People in organizations directly or tangentially related to your own, or those with the power to affect your own, will produce an impact. In order to leverage opportunities or meet present or future challenges, leaders must spend time on the external; for example, taking account of legal or political changes, trends (such as demographic or market), or technological advances. It's another element of strategy. In the best of organizations or for those leaders who are inherently outward-looking, this type of effort is seamless.

Try This

A basic review of the strength of your external orientation might be to think in terms of a gap analysis. With this, you can attempt to compare how your organization actually engages with the outside world and how you can better do so. Another way of considering the external is with the previously discussed "SWOT" analysis that captures strengths, weaknesses, opportunities, and threats.

In any case, if greater engagement is needed, consider dedicating more resources and making a sustained effort to adjust organizational culture. Some changes may be more easily executed than others; for example, those functions that by definition face outwards—customer outreach, public relations/affairs, and information/product sharing (e.g., through conferences, conventions, and symposiums).

Other efforts are more challenging; for example, those related to creating and managing or leading networks of people and organizations. Many contend this era of greater social connectedness and operational complexity requires a new dynamic to ensure maximum success. We as young leaders may be more equipped to operate in this collaborative environment, so don't hesitate to take charge.

5-Second Anecdote

Let's talk about a leader I call "We Have A Relationship Chip." I'll start out by saying that for most leaders, it's easier to address issues internal to work; they are right there staring you in the face. If you don't work them, it's also reasonable to think your boss and your peers will know. For issues external to the workplace, some leaders have different norms. Most leaders wouldn't act negligently, but it's true that stakeholders, contractors and others don't evaluate your performance. Often the external just doesn't rate. Enter Chip. He taught me that a leader is not doing their job if he or she doesn't provide strategic attention to external matters. In furtherance of any problem, Chip thought broadly. He wouldn't hesitate to invoke outside relationships he had built for the benefit of our unit or others in the organization. I can't tell you how many times I heard him say to another, "We have a relationship with them." It was an offer for Chip to contact that person or entity and advocate or inquire on something. As a good leader, Chip encouraged this type of engagement in others, bringing added focus to an important cause.

Consider Adaptive Management

Happy Hour Wisdom

Learn. Change. Repeat.

A Young Richard Branson

The Ugly Truth

Staying the course may be the right answer in some cases, but in others blindly doing more of the same can be a recipe for stagnation or failure. While the prospect of change can be difficult, a lack of flexibility can be disastrous.

The Bottom Line

Leaders embrace well-considered change as a means of maintaining organizational nimbleness on the path to success.

Try This

Building a methodology that includes flexibility in project or mission execution is crucial to adapting to indifferent market forces. We as young leaders need to be proactive agents of change so that change isn't later forced on us (or our replacements). It's instinctive, in a way. Dynamic, 360-degree-type-see-everything-that's-around-you, thinking requires a mechanism to alter decision-making and shift paradigms when the situation requires it. There is opportunity in this place. You want a strong, but agile, organization. The same goes for its leaders.

Adaptive management is often used in the context of creating environmental sustainability, but all organizations should strive for a framework that incorporates a learn-and-adapt mentality. This process is strategic in nature. You need to ask the right questions at the right time to generate provocative thought. In doing so, young leaders need to be bold in charting a course that may involve change.

5-Second Anecdote

I once had a leader, let's call him "Clean It Up Carl." Carl was ostensibly brought in to tidy up the messes of his predecessor. The person Carl replaced was a decent leader who oversaw some notable successes; however, he certainly did not make the organization sustainable (see "Fred" in "Have a Vision"). Carl came in and pushed a framework that connected people-focused initiatives (keep staff resourced, trained, rewarded) to properly executed projects, in the hopes that the two would drive each other. Carl understood that our organization's imminent future likely involved the prospect of significant change, and he wanted to set up a structure that could adapt to new challenges. The organization was all the better because of Carl's efforts.

Implement Organizational Change the Right Way

Happy Hour Wisdom

The reality of change is the only constant.

The Ugly Truth

As people are typically adverse to the uncertainty change creates, there is almost nothing more difficult or more important for a leader to manage than the shifting of fundamental workplace components such as goals, roles, processes, or organizational structure. People, individually, and organizations, cumulatively, do not like to change.

A Young Jeff Bezos

The Bottom Line

A nimble, dynamic organization that confronts challenges in a strategic way is better poised to achieve success. For this reason, we as young leaders must seek to manage change by working through the uncertainties in order to minimize staff anxiety, address resistance, and achieve the desired future state in an organized way.

Try This

If you're talking change management in your organization, presumably it has been preceded by a logical strategic planning or problem-solving effort. The next steps involve creating a change process that is well-planned, well-reasoned, and sensibly paced. Every step and all possible outcomes should be thought through.

Leaders must take care to lay the groundwork for change by methodically working through the unpredictable. Early on, understand and personally communicate to staff the genesis of the change and why it's important. Provide as much detail as possible (think "who," "what," "when," "where," "why," and "how"). Paint the need to change in vivid terms. Staff should be made to feel part of the dialogue, and any measures that could be taken to address their concerns or minimize impact should be considered.

Different employees will cope with change in different ways. Typical instincts tend towards the emotional, however, and be forewarned that a staff already inclined to mistrust leadership is primed to experience an even greater intensity of feelings. And though staff may acknowledge the coming change, they may not embrace it. Understanding the values and culture of your organization (see the following chapter) might provide some advance warning on what type of response to anticipate and how best to mitigate it.

A thorough analysis of the desired change will assist in identifying what type of staff engagement is needed. Be exacting. For example, training is important for teaching new requirements and skills that allow individuals to succeed at their present position. Development is the process of learning different or upgraded skills necessary to accomplish a new task or position. If skills need to be taught as a result of your planned change, which method is appropriate?

Finally, the giving and receiving of continual feedback between staff and leadership allows you to gauge the pace and success of implementation and identify needed course corrections. On the back end of implementation, seek to ensure goals have been achieved and change is permanently cemented.

Within many different leadership topics there exist models that simulate common challenges and issues. These are founded in academic research or executive management literature, and they provide much more specificity than you'll see in this book. The subject lesson on organizational change is a good example. The key here is for we as young leaders to recognize when a situation requires additional, more thorough review.

5-Second Anecdote

Let's talk about a leader named "Change-Minded Chet." Chet oversaw some impressive change within his unit over a remarkably short period of time. He implemented a new database, expanded his staff's geographic service area, and experienced a growth in business that increased workload. Chet's meticulous attention to detail in planning for and carrying out this change served him well. However, his sheer force of will was also a large part of his success—the change wasn't seamless, and his staff wasn't happy at first, but he consistently and deliberately provided guidance and follow-through. I mention Chet not because he possessed any secrets. Chet's adherence to the principles of change management is what made him successful, and that in itself is what made him extraordinary. To this day, he is one of the only positive examples of change management implementation to which I can point.

Understand Organizational Culture and Core Values

Happy Hour Wisdom

Value culture.

The Ugly Truth

Leaders use their intellect and instinct to interpret the organization and understand its soul. This effort usually requires deliberate inquiry and takes time and patience—don't rush it.

The Bottom Line

Organizations are like people—complex, emotional, and self-involved. Leaders need to understand this and act accordingly so they may appropriately interpret, respect, and, wherever possible, act in conformity with the norms that facilitate group cohesiveness. Doing so provides a better springboard to achieving mission success.

Try This*

Culture defines the organization as a group and is brought about by that which created it and that which continues to shape it. Culture can be difficult to articulate and therefore regarded as unknowable. There are, however, many ways for a young leader to go about piecing together this often-complex puzzle.

The heart of the inquiry is to define the elements of organizational culture. Values (i.e., beliefs), when joined with norms (i.e., standard social behaviors) and myths (i.e., stories groups share to interpret their experience and perpetuate their actions), produce culture.

Though we don't generally talk about them, values, norms, and myths are enforced and reinforced within organizations. Their continued propagation supports assumptions in the way business is conducted. Once you know what drives an organization, you can use that insight to do many things, including better implementing change or a strategic plan. The key is to use what you know to reflect respect for the positive values, norms, and myths of the organization—and steer clear of or properly mitigate actions that would implicate the negative values, norms, or myths.

One way to go about an examination of culture, generally, and those most important ("core") values, specifically, is to employ some critical distance between yourself and the organization and spend time thinking about what you see and hear. Consider: How does staff interact with one another? What motivates them? Is there a rhythm to the organization? At its best and at its worst, how does work get accomplished? What processes do staff use?

A Young Larry Page, Google Co-Founder

Think backwards as well and do some research if necessary. Solicit input from wise men and women of the organization who have been around awhile. Peruse organizational publications and see which types of stories are written and repeated. Ponder: What is the organization's history? For better and worse, how have key leaders affected it? Are there key successes and failures that have contributed to the collective memory of the organization? How has its unique mission shaped the way staff thinks and acts?

The act of considering culture allows young leaders to better calibrate and implement their decisions. Understand that there is a whole field of study involving organizational culture, and much more information and expertise is available when the need arises.

5-Second Anecdote

I didn't realize my organization had a culture until I began to discuss the subject with others out of concern for some recent morale issues. I learned from a few who had been around awhile that our culture was one of mission accomplishment, first, and concern for adherence to defined processes, second. And while we succeeded in executing our mission, we completed our workload unevenly—most often right before deadline. Staff could be driven to work hard for short periods but then suffered from exhaustion. Leader after leader reinforced or tacitly supported this culture because it worked—until we had become quite extreme in our behavior. We lacked any sense of moderation. Staff was anxious, frustrated, and overall, inefficient. Finally, we came across a senior leader who recognized we could be stronger. "Right Way Rita" respected our successes, but set about addressing challenges and improving on our accomplishments in a way that reflected an appropriate response to our culture.

---

*The following were reviewed in writing this section:
(1) Burke, C., Macdonald, I., and Stewart, K. "Structure is Not Enough: Systems are the Drivers of Organizational Behavior and Culture." In K. Shepard, J. Gray, J. Hunt, and S. McArthur (Eds.), Organization Design, Levels of Work & Human Capability: Executive Guide. (GO Reading Series 2007). pp.241-255
(2) National Defense University, Industrial College of the Armed Forces, Department of Strategic Decision Making and Executive Information Systems. Strategic Leadership and Decision-Making: Preparing Senior Executives for the 21st Century. (Government Printing Office, 1997)
(3) "Organizational Culture." Wikipedia: The Free Encyclopedia. Wikipedia Foundation, Inc. date last updated (08 September 2014). Web.

Be Prepared for a Crisis

Happy Hour Wisdom

Anticipate the unexpected.

The Ugly Truth

In times of crisis or emergency (used interchangeably here), leaders—and the resilience of the organizations they have built—are tested. The pass/fail consequence of this exam is as real-life as you will ever experience.

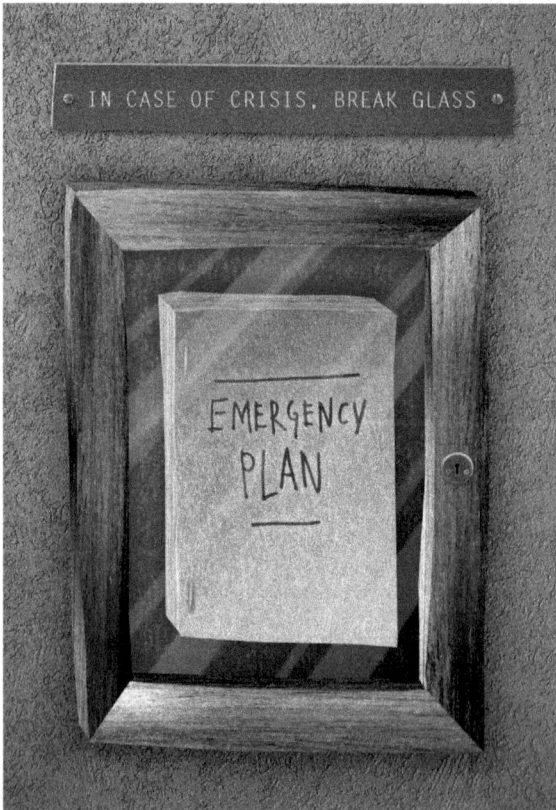

IN CASE OF CRISIS, BREAK GLASS

EMERGENCY PLAN

The Bottom Line

Crises are predictable—to an extent. You know something is going to happen...you just don't know what, when, and where. The organization may have some sort of disruption of operations, a loss of leadership, or financial difficulties. The issue may affect your very ability to lead. Regardless, success in surviving the most challenging of times requires a specific readiness and a resilient attitude.

Try This

Before a crisis occurs, a contingency operations plan covering most every imaginable event should be written, reviewed, and communicated to all appropriate staff. Hold meetings and exercises to ensure staff understands who is responsible for what actions when an urgent situation presents itself.

In the absence of crisis, maintain vigilance. Leaders should have a heightened sense that the unimaginable is always a possibility and should be able to move swiftly and seamlessly to engage any matter when it occurs. Complacency is more than just a lack of alertness. Organizational morass—leaders and staff unable to make good, quick decisions, with efficient implementation—poses a general danger even aside from the possibility that a crisis may occur. It indicates your organization may not possess the agility to handle a wide range of contingency events successfully.

During the crisis itself, leaders need to remain steadfast and calm. Be clear-headed and honest with yourself and others about the task at hand, and don't abandon the good habits of leadership just because of an emergency—simply expedite your action. Work in coordination with your most trusted advisors, but be prepared to actively manage operations and staff, perhaps more so than under normal circumstances. Also remember that leaders don't need to pretend to have all the answers, but they do need to be prepared to exercise good judgment and act decisively (even if that action is patience) as the situation requires.

Finally, it is probably a little cliché, but with crisis comes opportunity. That opportunity may be in the form of demonstrating leadership, uniting staff, rewarding performance, and even instituting change that would be too dramatic under normal circumstances. While working towards stabilizing the situation, be thinking ahead towards how you could make the best of the tumult.

There is a significant amount of study devoted to managing or leading during a crisis. Many organizations have staff or departments devoted entirely to this mission. Take the need to anticipate such an event seriously, and you may consider yourself prepared.

5-Second Anecdote

I have had the experience of participating in emergency preparedness and response at several organizations. The leadership lessons I learned during the actual crises—along with the incidents themselves—are among the most vivid of my young career. I remember working in a non-profit organization when a gunman stormed into the building, past security, and opened fire with an automatic weapon. There was no plan; we just took cover. Those of us who were able to do so barricaded our individual offices and called 9-1-1. We waited for the police, who arrived and shot the gunman. Amazingly, no staff was injured. Our actions during the chaos of that moment were proper, though we had not trained for such an event. An active shooter incident—an unhappy client seeking revenge—may be unlikely but not inconceivable, and we should have been better prepared. With decent judgment, quick action, and a little luck, however, we survived. It took many months of counseling to care for shaken staff, but we shared in the process of healing: we mourned the gunman's death, we celebrated the bravery of the police, and then we got back to work, together.

Don't Forget People

Happy Hour Wisdom

Handle others with care.

The Ugly Truth

People are the foundation and the heart of all organizations. If you neglect them, you risk their well-being and that of your enterprise.

The Bottom Line

This is really about putting it all together to provide for the needs of a healthy workforce. The goal is to motivate staff to succeed, and then match performance with reward.

Try This

Do a top-to-bottom evaluation of your organization's contribution to "people health." This requires both a personal and professional check-up. Key questions include the following: Do you provide staff with performance counseling to help them achieve their work and career objectives? Do you provide staff with the tools necessary to do their job (including not only material, but training and a safe working environment)? Is there a telework program? Are there resources available (such as emotional or financial support) for those in need? What about opportunities to team-build? How about physical fitness facilities? Do you provide childcare? Does the organization support volunteerism? For most, our time at work is a microcosm of our lives, and leaders should support this insofar as the ends contribute to physically and mentally healthy staff.

Leaders should also create other opportunities to motivate and appreciate. This is "golden rule"-type stuff. Come to know your staff as people: celebrate with them, mourn with them, and have fun with them. Respect staff well enough to be honest with them, even if it means providing them incomplete information, or if puts you or the organization in a bad light. Inspire staff—take the time to talk with them about how their role is connected to the organization's mission. Share with staff by communicating frequently on topics both large and small. Promote a balanced lifestyle. Keep your office door open—listen to staff concerns and work towards meeting their needs to the extent practicable.

Finally, regularly motivate staff through recognition. This may be small (a "thank you" or a "shout out") or through some larger, more public and generous award. And for staff who are motivated and perform well, take care not to overuse them to the point of burnout.

5-Second Anecdote

I learned the lessons of a people-focused leader relatively late in my young career. Prior to that, I experienced multiple extremes in senior leadership—shifts in temperament that variously damned or coddled staff—and this influenced my own thinking as to the proper balance between performance and reward. I knew a leader, let's call him "Insincere Ivan." Ivan talked a good game about caring for people, but his actions weren't sincere—and people knew it. He sprinkled reward amidst fear and manipulation, and he lacked moderation and propriety (he judged hastily and indiscreetly). Though he had set a nice table, the praise he conferred provided scant nourishment. Ivan wasn't taking care of staff—he was using them.

Part V. I'm Ready to Pay It Forward

There are many similarities between young, emerging leaders and their more experienced peers. Concentrated focus, hard work, and determination are required for everyone to get ahead, stay ahead, and get the job done right. A young leader—hopefully a little more enriched by the completion of this book—is perhaps more intensely focused on self-development as a means of ensuring mission accomplishment.

But a young leader is still a leader, and youth and inexperience should never be made an excuse for one's shortcomings. Hopefully, there would be no need. In enhancing a dialogue on leadership, individuals, communities, and organizations can move towards greater patience and support for a more mature, realistic approach to leader development and promotion. A greater understanding of what leadership is (and is not) can help us discuss how to move more deliberately towards overcoming our greatest challenges.

This book provides a range of advice on a variety of leadership components. The lessons are tools for you keep to at your side to assist in resolving issues as they arise. At a certain point during your journey—not at the beginning, but probably not too far from it—you will have an adequate amount of knowledge to begin sharing what you have learned with others. Recognizing you have reached this milestone is important.

Being a leader is unique in that, aside from execution, leaders have a duty to pass on their skills to others. From a CEO who writes a book (ostensibly passing on his or her wisdom), to a peer-to-peer discussion of a problem that has arisen on the factory floor, the sharing of knowledge is done all the time, in ways both large and small.

So, though you continue to self-develop, consider whether you are doing enough to make time to teach others. There are multiple reasons to devote yourself to this critical work.

First, it is as simple as succession-planning—you want good people to fill key vacancies (maybe even your own!). Protect your organization's future by ensuring that there are enough skilled, experienced individuals being trained to take on current and future responsibilities.

Second, leaders always rely on others to assist in executing their mission—the more you teach, the better your staff, the greater the chance of success. Don't make the mistake of protecting your own position by building a bench of people who are incapable of independent thought and action.

Finally, leaders need to teach others their craft because, though the field of leadership itself is broad, our challenges and the organizations that can address them are unique and specialized—ensuring an endless variety of niche lessons. That's why leaders emerge in every field: the politician-leader, the business-leader, the sports-leader, etc.

Considering the above, at some point you may be called upon—or feel compelled—to begin teaching others about how to enhance their leadership skills. The message here is that you should not hesitate to do so. Don't be modest. You don't need to know everything to begin to share your experience. Leadership is fluid. There are lessons to be learned and shared throughout one's experience—don't wait until you are old and gray to pass on a voluminous account of what you've learned.

One way to teach is via the buddy system. Find a peer, and learn and share together informally—over lunch, on breaks, while walking to a meeting.

Another way is to seek out junior staff as part of an informal or formal program to mentor others. If informal, you can be subtle: "I learned that the hard way ... if you want to grab lunch sometime, I can tell you what happened to me..."

A more formal way that some organizations develop their leaders is via a Leadership Development Program, with a select class, formal curriculum, and regular meeting schedule. This is one of the more concrete ways to build leadership skills continually within your organization. This type of program can be developed with internal resources—choose your best leaders to teach—or you can bring in consultants to develop and execute a program.

There is a certain virtue in teaching others, but learn to appreciate both the selfless and selfish implications. Leadership is about making things happen—for us, others, and for the greater good. Leadership doesn't just happen—but it *can* be learned. If you've read up to this page, you know that when I'm working, there is a lot going through my head: lots of mottos, lots of stories, lots of balancing, lots of concern. If you are a leader focused on success, your head should be filled. Often it's unmanageable; always, it's difficult.

It's also what you signed up for. It's a challenge, it's an opportunity. Doctors save lives. Pilots land planes. Leaders focus on, and achieve, the organization's mission. Everything you do must lead up to this end—so get out there and do it!

And after you cope with the issues laid out in this book, continue to challenge your own leadership skills for the purpose of moving to the next level of success. Recall that, beyond the words printed here, it's important to learn through observation, imitation, and on-the-job trial and error. Leaders don't call themselves leaders. Leaders humbly aspire to the role and are in a constant state of getting there.

Your business, community, and organization need a skillful, teaching 'you' to navigate a myriad of challenging issues during some very difficult times. Good luck, Godspeed, and happy leading. Enjoy the journey…that's where the pleasure lies!

Afterword

Picasso said "It is your work in life that is the ultimate seduction." I'm out there laboring, strategizing, dreaming, and continually seeking an outlet for my passions. I lie in wait for my next mission. And when opportunity comes, I want to leverage my influence-building skills to succeed.

Small changes, combined, make a difference. The future gives me hope because I know I'm not alone. There are many young people out there who have found their niche and are leading the way. And as the emerging generations that are producing today's young leaders increasingly lay claim to the collective responsibility of guiding our future, there is hope that tomorrow will look different...and better.

After 9/11, when I boarded the flight from JFK back to Los Angeles, I was motivated but still a bit naïve. I imagined, and I truly wanted to believe, that a leadership journey could be efficient and predictable. It's the optimist in me. But the journey ended up being tough at times and longer than I expected, and it was sometimes filled with uncomfortable lessons learned. I soldiered on, though, and you should too. As I said when I began this book, the story of leadership is that of opportunity lost and gained. The sum of the experiences that shape us, from the global to the local to the intensely personal, determine what we are capable of achieving. Leaders harness the best of themselves, layer-in what they learn, and set out to make a difference. Be that person!

Appendix

CRIB SHEET

Lesson Name:_____

My **take away** from this lesson is...

_____
_____
_____
_____
_____
_____
_____
_____
_____
_____

I want to start or stop doing the following in the **short term**...

_____
_____
_____
_____
_____
_____
_____
_____
_____
_____

I am going to **implement** this change by doing the following...

_____
_____
_____
_____
_____
_____
_____
_____
_____
_____

I want to start or stop doing the following in the **long term**...

_____
_____
_____
_____
_____
_____
_____
_____

I am going to **implement** this change by doing the following...

_____
_____
_____
_____
_____
_____
_____
_____

I disagree with what I've read, because I think that...

_____
_____
_____
_____
_____
_____
_____
_____

I have some questions and need to **think about / research**...

_____
_____
_____
_____
_____
_____
_____

www.ingramcontent.com/pod-product-compliance
Lightning Source LLC
Chambersburg PA
CBHW060036210326
41520CB00009B/1151